React Native for Mobile Development: Build Cross-Platform Apps

A Complete Guide to Developing Mobile Apps with React Native

MIGUEL FARMER

RAFAEL SANDERS

Table of Content

TABLE OF CONTENTS

INTRODUCTION

React Native for Mobile and Web Development

Welcome to **"React Native for Mobile and Web Development: A Complete Guide to Building Cross-Platform Apps"**. This book is designed to help developers harness the power of **React Native**—an open-source framework for building mobile apps with a single codebase that works on both **iOS** and **Android**. Whether you're new to React Native or looking to expand your knowledge, this book provides a comprehensive, hands-on guide to building high-quality, performant mobile and web apps using React Native.

React Native has quickly become one of the most popular choices for mobile app development. It allows you to write applications using **JavaScript** and **React**, but instead of being confined to the web browser, it lets you write mobile applications that feel truly native. With **React Native for Web**, you can now extend the power of React Native beyond mobile apps and create applications that run seamlessly across iOS, Android, and web platforms.

In this book, we will cover all aspects of React Native development, from the basics of setting up your development environment to advanced topics like **state management with Redux**, **native integration**, and **working with third-party APIs**.

By the end of this book, you will have the skills to build powerful and scalable applications for mobile and the web with React Native.

Who This Book is For

This book is aimed at developers who want to learn **React Native** and how to build cross-platform apps using this framework. Whether you are an experienced developer already familiar with JavaScript, React, or mobile development, or a beginner just starting out, this book will provide the knowledge and tools you need to build real-world applications.

- **Beginner developers**: If you're new to mobile development or React, you'll find this book to be a step-by-step guide to building your first mobile and web apps with React Native.
- **Intermediate developers**: If you already have some experience with React and mobile app development, this book will help you deepen your understanding of React Native and introduce you to advanced concepts like native modules, state management, and performance optimization.
- **Web developers**: If you're already familiar with React for web development, this book will show you how to

extend your knowledge to build apps for mobile platforms using React Native, as well as build web apps using **React Native for Web**.

What You Will Learn

This book is organized into several parts, each covering a key area of React Native development. Let's take a closer look at what you will learn:

- **Part 1: Introduction to React Native and Setting Up Your Development Environment**
  In the first part, we'll introduce **React Native**, set up your development environment, and help you get started with your first project. You will learn about the architecture of React Native, how to write your first app, and how to test it on both mobile and web platforms.

- **Part 2: React Native Fundamentals**
  We will dive into the core building blocks of React Native, including how to work with components, styling, and layout. You will learn how to manage app state, handle navigation between screens, and interact with APIs.

- **Part 3: Building Real-World Apps with React Native**
  You will build fully-functional apps with **React Native**,

including a **shopping cart app**, a **fitness tracker**, and a **social media app**. These hands-on projects will help you learn how to handle data, manage state with **Redux**, and integrate native mobile features into your apps.

- **Part 4: Advanced Topics in React Native**
  This section covers advanced topics such as **native modules**, **native UI components**, and **integrating complex native features** into your app. You will learn how to extend React Native with custom views and access platform-specific APIs for a truly native experience.

- **Part 5: State Management and Performance Optimization**
  In this part, we explore **Redux**, one of the most widely used libraries for managing application state in React and React Native. We'll also cover performance optimization techniques and show you how to make your React Native apps run smoothly, even when handling complex interactions.

- **Part 6: Deploying and Publishing Your App**
  Finally, we'll guide you through the process of **deploying** and **publishing** your app to the **Google Play Store** and **Apple App Store**, as well as deploying a React Native web app to the web. You will learn how to handle app configurations, app icons, splash screens, and submission processes.

- **Part 7: Real-World Project Examples**
Throughout the book, we will build **real-world projects**
such as an **e-commerce app**, **fitness tracking app**, and
social media platform, demonstrating how to implement
features such as **GPS tracking, step counting, workout
logs**, and **payment gateway integration**. These projects
will give you hands-on experience in building functional
and scalable apps using React Native.

Key Features of This Book

- **Hands-on Projects**: This book includes step-by-step
instructions to build real-world apps, including a
shopping cart, fitness tracker, social media app, and more.
You will apply the concepts you've learned to build fully-
functional applications.
- **Cross-Platform Development**: React Native allows you
to build apps that run on **both mobile (iOS and Android)**
and **the web**. We will show you how to set up and manage
projects that target all these platforms, and even build a
universal React Native app for mobile and web.
- **State Management with Redux**: We will cover how to
manage complex app states using **Redux**, one of the most
widely-used libraries in the React ecosystem. This will
help you build scalable, maintainable apps.

- **Advanced Topics**: The book also explores advanced concepts like **native modules, native UI components,** and how to integrate these features into your React Native projects. You'll learn how to interact with native code and APIs to create custom functionality.

- **Optimizing Performance**: You'll learn how to optimize your React Native apps to ensure they are fast and responsive, even when working with complex state and data.

How This Book is Structured

Each chapter builds on the last, with progressively more complex topics covered. We'll start by helping you set up your development environment and understanding the basics of React Native. Then, we'll guide you through building your first app and teach you how to manage state with Redux. You will then work through real-world examples that demonstrate how to integrate native functionality and optimize performance.

By the end of this book, you will have a comprehensive understanding of **React Native** and how to build **cross-platform applications** that run on mobile devices and the web. You'll have the skills to tackle complex projects and extend React Native to suit your needs, whether you're working on a small hobby project or building a large-scale production app.

Why This Book is Important

As the demand for mobile apps grows, React Native has emerged as a powerful tool for building apps that work on both iOS and Android with a single codebase. But with **React Native for Web**, it's now possible to use that same codebase to target the web as well. This book empowers you to make the most out of React Native's versatility, creating apps that can reach a broader audience across multiple platforms.

Whether you're a seasoned mobile developer or a web developer looking to expand into mobile, this book provides a solid foundation for mastering **React Native** and building cross-platform apps efficiently.

Conclusion

We're excited to take you on this learning journey through React Native. This book will equip you with the tools you need to create beautiful, functional, and performant mobile and web apps. Whether you are building your first mobile app or scaling an existing one, **React Native** offers the flexibility and power you need to build cutting-edge applications. Let's dive in and start building apps that work across platforms with React Native!

Part 1

Introduction to React Native and Mobile Development

CHAPTER 1

INTRODUCTION TO MOBILE DEVELOPMENT AND REACT NATIVE

Overview of Mobile Development

Mobile development refers to the process of creating software applications that run on mobile devices such as smartphones and tablets. Mobile apps can generally be categorized into two types: **native** apps and **web apps**. Over the years, mobile development has evolved significantly, with new frameworks and tools emerging to streamline the process of building apps for diverse platforms.

Historically, mobile development focused on **native development**, where developers would write platform-specific code for Android (Java) or iOS (Objective-C or Swift). While this approach allowed for high performance and deep integration with device features, it also led to the challenge of maintaining separate codebases for each platform. This gave rise to **cross-platform development**, which offers the ability to write code once and deploy it on multiple platforms, significantly reducing development time and cost.

Cross-Platform Development vs. Native Development

In mobile app development, there are two main approaches for building mobile apps:

1. Native Development

- **What is it?** Native development refers to building apps using platform-specific languages and tools. For **Android**, this would mean using **Java** or **Kotlin**; for **iOS**, this would mean using **Objective-C** or **Swift**.
- **Advantages**:
    - High performance due to direct access to device hardware and optimized code.
    - Full access to device-specific features (camera, sensors, GPS, etc.).
    - Native user interface elements provide a seamless user experience.
- **Disadvantages**:
    - Requires separate codebases for each platform (Android and iOS).

17

o Increased development time and cost since developers must write and maintain different code for each platform.
o Difficulties in ensuring consistency across platforms.

2. Cross-Platform Development

- **What is it?** Cross-platform development involves building mobile apps that can run on multiple platforms (Android and iOS) from a single codebase. Popular cross-platform frameworks include **React Native**, **Flutter**, and **Xamarin**.
- **Advantages**:
  o A single codebase for both Android and iOS reduces development time and cost.
  o The app's core business logic can be shared between platforms.
  o Faster updates and easier maintenance.
- **Disadvantages**:
  o Performance may not be as optimized as native apps in some cases.
  o Limited access to some device-specific features or APIs.
  o The user interface may not always match the platform's native design guidelines exactly.

18

What is React Native and Why It's Gaining Popularity

React Native is a JavaScript framework developed by **Facebook** for building cross-platform mobile applications. It allows developers to build mobile apps using **React**, a popular JavaScript library for building user interfaces, and **native components** for rendering platform-specific views. React Native bridges the gap between native code and JavaScript, allowing developers to write most of their app logic in JavaScript while still leveraging native performance and capabilities.

Why is React Native gaining popularity?

- **Single Codebase for Multiple Platforms**: One of React Native's greatest strengths is the ability to write a single codebase for both Android and iOS, making it an attractive option for developers looking to save time and reduce costs.

- **Performance**: React Native compiles to native code, meaning it provides near-native performance for most applications. Although performance may not always match fully native apps, React Native's performance is generally sufficient for the majority of apps.

- **Familiarity with React**: React Native allows JavaScript developers who are already familiar with React to transition to mobile app development without learning

19

new languages or frameworks. This makes it an easy and natural step for web developers to extend their skills into mobile development.

- **Large Community and Ecosystem**: React Native is backed by Facebook and has a large, active community. This means that developers can easily find resources, libraries, and tools to speed up development. It also enjoys regular updates and improvements.

- **Hot Reloading**: React Native's hot reloading feature allows developers to instantly see the effects of code changes without recompiling the entire app, greatly improving the development process.

Advantages and Limitations of React Native

Advantages of React Native:

- **Faster Development**: Since it allows for a shared codebase across both platforms, React Native speeds up the development process. Developers can write components once and reuse them, reducing time spent on building for each platform separately.

- **Native Performance**: React Native uses native components for rendering UI elements, which ensures the app has a high-performance level comparable to that of native apps.

- **Community Support**: Being open-source and backed by Facebook, React Native enjoys strong community support. The ecosystem is rich with third-party libraries, tools, and resources that make development easier and faster.

- **Third-Party Plugin Support**: React Native has robust support for third-party libraries and plugins, including those that give access to device features (like the camera, GPS, etc.) and integrate with existing native code when necessary.

- **Cross-Platform Consistency**: React Native provides tools like **React Navigation** to ensure your app looks and behaves similarly on both Android and iOS, with customizations available for platform-specific UI patterns.

Limitations of React Native:

- **Limited Native Module Support**: While React Native has access to many native modules, there are still instances where certain device-specific features may require custom native code. This can result in the need for additional development or integration with platform-specific libraries.

- **Performance for Complex Apps**: Although React Native offers good performance for most apps, extremely performance-sensitive apps (such as high-end games or

21

intensive graphical apps) might still require native development.

- **Native Code Integration**: While React Native allows integration with native code, this can introduce complexity in your app's architecture. In cases where you need deep integration with the operating system, you might still need to rely on native development.

- **Frequent Updates**: As React Native evolves rapidly, some libraries or tools may become deprecated or require frequent updates to stay compatible with newer versions of React Native or the platforms themselves.

Real-World Example: React Native in Popular Apps

React Native is used in several large-scale, high-performance applications, proving its capability to handle production-level apps with millions of users. Here are a few well-known examples:

1. Facebook:

- Facebook developed React Native to address their challenge of maintaining separate teams for Android and iOS development. They created React Native to unify the development process while still providing native performance and flexibility. Today, Facebook uses React

Native to maintain their mobile apps and even for building new features.

2. Instagram:

- Instagram, also owned by Facebook, was one of the early adopters of React Native. The app uses React Native to quickly build and deliver new features across both Android and iOS. React Native helped Instagram reduce development time for cross-platform features like Push Notifications, Live Video, and new user-facing features.

3. Airbnb:

- Airbnb used React Native in its mobile app to speed up development and maintenance. Initially, Airbnb used React Native to build features like the user profile and listings. However, due to challenges with complex navigation and performance in certain areas, Airbnb eventually moved away from React Native for some parts of the app. Nonetheless, the app's use of React Native was still a significant success story for cross-platform development.

4. Uber Eats:

- Uber Eats uses React Native for parts of their mobile app, particularly in the restaurant interface and order tracking features. This approach allowed Uber Eats to have a shared codebase for both iOS and Android while still maintaining high performance.

These examples demonstrate that React Native is capable of supporting large-scale, performance-intensive applications, while also improving development speed and efficiency.

Conclusion

In this chapter, we've introduced you to the world of mobile development and how React Native is changing the way we approach building cross-platform mobile apps. By providing a unified framework for both Android and iOS, React Native offers a powerful solution for developers looking to build efficient, scalable, and high-performance apps with a single codebase.

In the following chapters, we'll delve deeper into the React Native ecosystem, covering everything from setting up your development environment to building and deploying real-world apps. By the end of this book, you will have the skills and knowledge necessary to confidently build and deploy mobile apps using React Native.

Let's get started!

CHAPTER 2

SETTING UP THE DEVELOPMENT ENVIRONMENT

In this chapter, we'll walk through the process of setting up the development environment for React Native. You'll install all the necessary tools and configure both Android and iOS emulators, ensuring that you are ready to begin building cross-platform mobile apps with React Native.

Installing Node.js, npm, and React Native CLI

Before you can start working with React Native, you'll need to install **Node.js**, **npm (Node Package Manager),** and the **React Native CLI**. These tools are essential for running JavaScript code and managing packages in React Native projects.

Step 1: Install Node.js

Node.js is a JavaScript runtime that lets you run JavaScript on your machine, outside of a web browser. React Native uses Node.js to handle various development tasks, such as running the packager and managing dependencies.

25

1. Go to the Node.js official website and download the latest **LTS** (Long Term Support) version.

2. Follow the installation instructions for your operating system.

3. Once installed, you can verify the installation by opening a terminal/command prompt and running the following commands:

```bash

node -v
npm -v

```

These commands will display the installed versions of Node.js and npm, confirming that the installation was successful.

Step 2: Install React Native CLI

The **React Native CLI** is a command-line interface used to create and manage React Native projects. While there is also a package called **Expo** for React Native, we'll be using the React Native CLI to give us full control over the build process and access to native code.

1. Open a terminal or command prompt and run the following command to install the React Native CLI globally:

```
bash
```

```
npm install -g react-native-cli
```

The -g flag installs the package globally, making the react-native command available system-wide.

2. Verify that React Native CLI is installed correctly by running:

```
bash
```

```
react-native --version
```

This should display the version of React Native CLI installed.

Setting up Android Studio and Xcode for Emulator Support

To run and test your React Native apps, you'll need to set up emulators for both Android and iOS. Emulators simulate real mobile devices on your computer, allowing you to test your apps without needing a physical device.

Step 3: Setting up Android Studio for Android Emulator

1. **Download Android Studio**: Visit the Android Studio website and download the installer for your operating system.

2. **Install Android Studio**: Follow the installation instructions provided for your operating system. Make sure to install the **Android SDK, Android Virtual Device (AVD)**, and **Android Emulator** during the setup process.

3. **Configure Android Studio**:
   o Launch **Android Studio**.
   o Open the **AVD Manager** (found under the **Tools** menu).
   o Create a new Android Virtual Device (AVD) by selecting a device model (such as Pixel 3) and a system image (such as the latest Android version).
   o Once the emulator is set up, you can start it by clicking on the play icon in the AVD Manager.

4. **Set up the Android environment variables**: To ensure React Native can find Android Studio and the AVD, you need to set the ANDROID_HOME environment variable.
   o On **macOS**/Linux, add the following to your .bash_profile or .zshrc file:

   bash

28

```
export
ANDROID_HOME=$HOME/Library/Android/
sdk
export
PATH=$ANDROID_HOME/tools:$ANDROID_H
OME/platform-tools:$PATH
```

- On **Windows**, add the following to your system environment variables:

```
bash
```

```
ANDROID_HOME    =    C:\Users\<Your-
Username>\AppData\Local\Android\Sdk
```

5. **Verify Android setup**: Run the following command to check if Android Studio and the Android SDK are set up correctly:

```
bash
```

```
adb devices
```

If this shows a list of devices or emulators, then you are ready to proceed.

Step 4: Setting up Xcode for iOS Emulator (macOS only)

If you're developing on **macOS** and wish to run your React Native app on an iOS simulator, you need to set up **Xcode**, which is Apple's integrated development environment (IDE) for iOS and macOS.

1. **Install Xcode**:
   - Download **Xcode** from the Mac App Store.
   - Once installed, open **Xcode** and complete any initial setup steps.
2. **Install Command Line Tools**:
   - Open a terminal and run:

```bash
```

```
xcode-select --install
```

3. This installs the necessary command-line tools for building iOS applications.
4. **Set up iOS Simulator**:
   - Open **Xcode** and navigate to **Xcode > Preferences > Components**.
   - Install the desired version of the iOS simulator.
   - To start the simulator, use **Xcode > Open Developer Tool > Simulator**.
5. **Verify Xcode setup**: To ensure Xcode is correctly set up, run the following command:

```bash
xcode-select -p
```

This should return the path to Xcode's installation directory.

Initializing Your First React Native Project

Once the development environment is set up, you can initialize your first React Native project.

Step 5: Create a New React Native Project

1. **Create a new project**: In your terminal, navigate to the directory where you want to create your project and run the following command:

```bash
npx react-native init HelloWorld
```

This will create a new React Native project called HelloWorld with all the necessary files and configurations.

2. **Navigate to the project directory**:

31

```bash
cd HelloWorld
```

3. **Run the app on Android**: To run your app on an Android emulator, use the following command:

```bash
npx react-native run-android
```

4. **Run the app on iOS** (macOS only): To run your app on an iOS simulator, use the following command:

```bash
npx react-native run-ios
```

5. **Check if the app works**: After running the app, you should see the default React Native welcome screen on the emulator. This confirms that everything is working correctly.

Real-World Example: Setting up a Basic "Hello World" App

To verify that your React Native setup is working properly, let's set up a simple **"Hello World"** app.

1. **Modify the App.js file**: Open the App.js file in the project directory and replace its contents with the following:

```javascript
import React from 'react';
import { SafeAreaView, Text, StyleSheet } from 'react-native';

const App = () => {
  return (
    <SafeAreaView style={styles.container}>
      <Text style={styles.text}>Hello World!</Text>
    </SafeAreaView>
  );
};

const styles = StyleSheet.create({
  container: {
    flex: 1,
    justifyContent: 'center',
    alignItems: 'center',
    backgroundColor: '#fff',
  },
  text: {
    fontSize: 20,
```

```
    fontWeight: 'bold',
  },
});


export default App;
```

2. **Run the app**:

   o If you're using **Android**, use `npx react-native run-android`.

   o If you're on **macOS** and using **iOS**, use `npx react-native run-ios`.

Once the app loads on the emulator, you'll see the message **"Hello World!"** displayed at the center of the screen.

Conclusion

In this chapter, you've successfully set up the development environment for building React Native apps. You installed the necessary tools, including Node.js, npm, and React Native CLI, configured Android Studio and Xcode for emulator support, and created and ran your first React Native project.

Now that you have the foundation set up, you are ready to dive deeper into React Native and start building your own mobile apps. In the upcoming chapters, we will explore more advanced features like navigation, state management, and integrating APIs, helping you create robust and dynamic mobile applications.

CHAPTER 3

REACT NATIVE ARCHITECTURE

In this chapter, we will explore the core architecture of React Native, focusing on how it bridges the gap between JavaScript code and native code, and how these two worlds interact seamlessly to create mobile applications. We will also discuss the threading model used in React Native, which is key to understanding its performance and how it manages UI updates and complex tasks.

Understanding the Core Architecture of React Native

React Native is a framework that allows you to build mobile applications using JavaScript and React. However, React Native doesn't just run JavaScript code—it also communicates directly with native code to leverage the native capabilities of mobile devices. To achieve this, React Native uses a unique architecture that consists of several key components:

1. **JavaScript Code**:
   o This is where you write your business logic and UI components. JavaScript handles the app's

logic, interacts with APIs, and manages the user interface via React components.

- o React Native uses **React** to structure the UI, but the actual rendering happens through native components (UI elements specific to iOS and Android).

2. **Native Modules**:
   - o React Native gives you access to platform-specific APIs (e.g., camera, location services, sensors, etc.) by providing **native modules**. These modules allow your JavaScript code to interact with native code written in Java (for Android) or Swift/Objective-C (for iOS).

3. **Bridge**:
   - o The **Bridge** is a critical component that connects the JavaScript code with native modules. It is responsible for passing messages and data back and forth between the JavaScript thread and the native thread.

4. **Native Components**:
   - o These are UI elements native to the platform. For example, in iOS, a `<Text>` component is rendered as a native `UILabel`, and on Android, it's rendered as a native `TextView`.

The Bridge Concept and How It Communicates with Native Code

The **Bridge** is the mechanism that allows React Native to communicate between the JavaScript code and the native code. JavaScript and native code run in separate threads, and the Bridge facilitates the transfer of data between them.

How the Bridge Works:

- **JavaScript Thread**: This is where the JavaScript code runs. It contains the business logic and handles user interactions, such as responding to touch events.
- **Native Thread**: This is where the native code runs. It handles rendering the UI and interacts with the device's hardware (camera, GPS, sensors, etc.).
- **Bridge Communication**: Since JavaScript and native code are running on different threads, communication between them happens asynchronously through the Bridge. The Bridge transfers data and commands between these two threads.

Example of Bridge Communication:

1. **JS to Native**: When a JavaScript function (e.g., a user presses a button) triggers an event that requires native functionality (such as opening the camera), the JavaScript thread sends a message to the Native thread via the

38

Bridge. The Native thread then processes this and performs the necessary action.

2. **Native to JS**: When the native code needs to send data back to the JavaScript thread (such as data from the camera or a GPS location), it communicates back through the Bridge.

This asynchronous communication ensures that the JavaScript thread and the native thread do not block each other, allowing the app to remain responsive.

Understanding JavaScript Thread, Native Thread, and the Interaction

React Native uses a multi-threaded architecture, with distinct threads for JavaScript and native code. Here's how the two threads interact:

JavaScript Thread:

- This is where all your React code runs. It handles UI logic, state management, and event handling. In React Native, the JavaScript thread is responsible for executing business logic written in JavaScript.
- The JavaScript thread is single-threaded, meaning that if it gets blocked (for example, by a complex calculation or

a heavy loop), the app's performance can suffer. This is why performance optimization in React Native focuses on offloading tasks to the native thread whenever possible.

Native Thread:

- The native thread is responsible for rendering the UI and interacting with the device's hardware. For example, if you want to use the camera, the native thread will send a request to the camera's native module, which will then trigger the native code to open the camera and handle the output.
- The native thread is more suited to tasks that require heavy computations or interactions with the device hardware. React Native lets you offload complex tasks to the native thread to avoid blocking the JavaScript thread.

How They Interact:

1. **UI Updates**: When an action happens (e.g., a button click), React Native updates the JavaScript thread, which in turn tells the Native thread to update the UI.
2. **Asynchronous Communication**: The JavaScript thread and the native thread communicate asynchronously through the Bridge. This allows for a smooth, responsive experience, as both threads can operate independently without blocking one another.

3. **Thread Synchronization**: React Native handles synchronization between the threads. For example, when JavaScript requests native code to fetch data, the data will be sent back to the JavaScript thread once the native thread finishes processing. This data is passed asynchronously, which means the app continues running without delay.

Real-World Example: How React Native Interacts with Native UI Components

Let's consider a practical example where React Native interacts with native UI components: **displaying a native camera preview** within a React Native app.

Scenario: Building a Simple Camera App

You want to create a mobile app that allows users to take pictures using the phone's camera. React Native provides a module to interact with the native camera.

1. **Step 1: Requesting Camera Access from JavaScript**
   In your React Native code, you write a button that, when pressed, triggers the camera module:

   ```
   javascript
   ```

41

```
import React from 'react';
import { Button, View } from 'react-
native';
import { Camera } from 'react-native-
camera';

const CameraApp = () => {
  const openCamera = () => {
    // Call native code to open the camera
    Camera.open();
  };

  return (
    <View>
      <Button title="Open Camera"
onPress={openCamera} />
    </View>
  );
};

export default CameraApp;
```

- o **JavaScript Thread**: This code runs in the JavaScript thread and triggers the native camera module when the user presses the "Open Camera" button.

2. **Step 2: The Camera Module (Native Code)**
When the JavaScript thread calls `Camera.open()`, it sends a message to the **native thread** via the Bridge. This

42

message tells the native camera module to open the camera and show the camera preview on the screen.

- o **Native Thread**: The camera preview is rendered using native UI components (e.g., `UIImageView` on iOS or `SurfaceView` on Android), which are optimized for performance and native integration.

3. **Step 3: Handling the Camera Output**
   Once the user takes a photo, the camera module will send the photo data back to the JavaScript thread through the Bridge. The JavaScript thread can then handle the photo data, update the UI, or send the image to a server.

   - o **JavaScript Thread**: After receiving the photo data, you can display it in an image component or store it in the app's state.

Real-World Impact:

In this example, React Native allows you to write JavaScript to control the camera module, while relying on the native thread to render the camera preview and handle device-specific features. This separation of concerns ensures that React Native apps can leverage the full capabilities of mobile devices without sacrificing performance or usability.

Conclusion

In this chapter, we explored the core architecture of React Native, focusing on the Bridge concept, which enables seamless communication between JavaScript and native code. Understanding the interaction between the **JavaScript thread** and the **native thread** is crucial for optimizing performance and ensuring smooth user experiences in your React Native applications.

By leveraging the power of native components and offloading complex tasks to the native thread, React Native allows developers to create high-performance mobile applications with the flexibility of JavaScript. In the following chapters, we will dive deeper into how to use React Native's built-in modules to access device features, handle user input, and build dynamic UIs for your mobile apps.

Part 2

Fundamentals of React Native Development

CHAPTER 4

REACT COMPONENTS AND JSX
IN REACT NATIVE

Understanding Components in React Native

At the heart of React Native development is the concept of **components**. In React Native, everything you build is a component—whether it's a button, a text field, or an entire screen. Components are the building blocks of the user interface (UI), and they allow you to break down your UI into reusable, self-contained units of functionality.

What Are Components?

A component is a function or class that takes **props** (properties) as input and returns a piece of the UI (usually in the form of JSX, which is a syntactic extension of JavaScript). Components can be **stateful** or **stateless**, meaning they can either manage their own internal state or simply display data passed in through props.

There are two main types of components in React Native:

1. **Functional Components**:

46

- o These are simple JavaScript functions that return JSX.
- o They are often used for presentational purposes and don't typically manage their own state (though with the introduction of **React hooks**, functional components can now manage state as well).

2. **Class Components**:
   - o These are ES6 classes that extend `React.Component` and contain a `render` method to return JSX.
   - o Class components were the original way to write components in React, but with the introduction of React hooks, functional components have become the preferred way to write components.

In this chapter, we will cover both functional and class-based components and how they are used to create the UI in React Native.

Writing Functional and Class-Based Components

1. Functional Components

Functional components are the simplest type of component in React Native. They are defined as JavaScript functions that accept `props` as an argument and return JSX.

47

Example: Simple Functional Component

```javascript
import React from 'react';
import { Text, View } from 'react-native';

const WelcomeMessage = () => {
  return (
    <View>
      <Text>Hello, welcome to React Native!</Text>
    </View>
  );
};

export default WelcomeMessage;
```

- **Explanation**:
    o The component `WelcomeMessage` is a function that returns JSX, which consists of a `Text` component wrapped in a `View` component.
    o `Text` is a built-in React Native component used to display text.
    o `View` is another built-in component used as a container for other components.

      o You can use **props** to pass data into the component, although this example doesn't use props.

2. Class-Based Components

Class-based components are more powerful as they allow for managing **state**, lifecycle methods, and event handling. These components are created by extending `React.Component` and overriding the `render` method.

Example: Simple Class-Based Component

javascript

```
import React, { Component } from 'react';
import { Text, View } from 'react-native';

class WelcomeMessage extends Component {
  render() {
    return (
      <View>
        <Text>Hello, welcome to React Native from
a class-based component!</Text>
      </View>
    );
  }
}
```

```
export default WelcomeMessage;
```

- **Explanation**:
  - ○ `WelcomeMessage` is a class that extends `React.Component`. Inside the class, the `render` method returns the JSX that should be rendered on the screen.
  - ○ Class components have lifecycle methods, like `componentDidMount`, which we will explore later when dealing with more complex logic.

State in Class Components

Class components manage state using the `this.state` object and `this.setState()` method to update the state. Here's an example of a class component with state:

Example: Class-Based Component with State

javascript

```javascript
import React, { Component } from 'react';
import { Button, Text, View } from 'react-native';

class Counter extends Component {
  constructor(props) {
    super(props);
    this.state = {
```

50

```
      count: 0,
    };
  }


  increment = () => {
    this.setState({ count: this.state.count + 1
});
  };


  render() {
    return (
      <View>
        <Text>Count: {this.state.count}</Text>
        <Button              title="Increment"
onPress={this.increment} />
      </View>
    );
  }
}

export default Counter;
```

- **Explanation**:
  - The Counter class has a state property count, initialized to 0.
  - The increment method updates the state using this.setState().

o The `Button` component listens for a press event, which calls `this.increment` and updates the count.

State in Functional Components

Functional components now support state management through React Hooks. The `useState` hook is used to add state to functional components.

Example: Functional Component with State Using `useState` Hook

```javascript
import React, { useState } from 'react';
import { Button, Text, View } from 'react-
native';

const Counter = () => {
  const [count, setCount] = useState(0);

  const increment = () => {
    setCount(count + 1);
  };

  return (
    <View>
      <Text>Count: {count}</Text>
```

52

```
      <Button                        title="Increment"
onPress={increment} />
    </View>
  );
};


export default Counter;
```

- **Explanation**:
  - o The `useState` hook initializes the `count` variable and provides the `setCount` function to update it.
  - o When the `Button` is pressed, the `increment` function updates the `count` state, causing the component to re-render with the updated value.

JSX Syntax and How It Is Different from HTML

JSX (JavaScript XML) is a syntax extension for JavaScript that looks similar to HTML but is used in JavaScript code. React Native uses JSX to describe the UI structure, but there are some key differences between JSX and traditional HTML.

Key Differences Between JSX and HTML:

1. **Self-closing Tags**:

o In JSX, all tags must be closed. For example, `<input />` instead of `<input>`.

2. **Class vs. className**:

   o In HTML, we use `class` to define a class for an element. In JSX, you use `className` because `class` is a reserved keyword in JavaScript.

jsx

```jsx
<View className="container"></View>
```

3. **JavaScript Expressions**:

   o In JSX, you can embed JavaScript expressions inside curly braces `{ }`. This allows you to inject dynamic values or logic directly into the UI.

jsx

```jsx
const name = 'John';
<Text>Hello, {name}!</Text>
```

4. **Event Handling**:

   o In JSX, event handlers are written in camelCase, unlike HTML where they are written in lowercase.

jsx

```jsx
<Button onPress={handlePress} />
```

5. **Style**:

> o   In React Native, styles are written in JavaScript objects using **StyleSheet**. In HTML, styles are defined in CSS.

```jsx
const styles = StyleSheet.create({
  container: {
    flex: 1,
    justifyContent: 'center',
    alignItems: 'center',
    backgroundColor: '#fff',
  },
});

<View style={styles.container}></View>
```

Real-World Example: Creating a Basic User Interface Using Components

Let's build a simple **"Profile"** page UI using React Native components. The app will display a profile picture, name, and a short bio. We'll use **functional components**, **JSX**, and **styles** to create this layout.

Example: Profile Page UI

```javascript
javascript

import React from 'react';
import { View, Text, Image, StyleSheet } from
'react-native';

const Profile = () => {
  return (
    <View style={styles.container}>
      <Image
        source={{                              uri:
'https://placekitten.com/200/200' }}
        style={styles.image}
      />
      <Text style={styles.name}>John Doe</Text>
      <Text    style={styles.bio}>A    passionate
mobile developer.</Text>
    </View>
  );
};

const styles = StyleSheet.create({
  container: {
    flex: 1,
    justifyContent: 'center',
    alignItems: 'center',
    backgroundColor: '#f8f8f8',
  },
  image: {
```

```
    width: 150,
    height: 150,
    borderRadius: 75,
    marginBottom: 20,
  },
  name: {
    fontSize: 24,
    fontWeight: 'bold',
  },
  bio: {
    fontSize: 16,
    color: 'gray',
  },
});


export default Profile;
```

- **Explanation**:
    - ○ The component `Profile` uses JSX to structure the UI with an `Image`, two `Text` components, and a `View` container.
    - ○ **Image**: Displays a profile picture from a URL.
    - ○ **Text**: Displays the user's name and bio.
    - ○ **StyleSheet**: A `StyleSheet` is used to apply styles to the components. This allows for a clean and maintainable code structure.

Conclusion

In this chapter, we covered the fundamental building blocks of React Native: **components** and **JSX**. You learned how to create both **functional** and **class-based** components, how to manage **state** within components, and how JSX syntax differs from regular HTML. By using components, React Native allows you to create reusable and dynamic user interfaces, which is essential for building robust and scalable mobile applications.

Now that you understand how components work in React Native, you can start building more complex UIs by combining and customizing components. In the next chapters, we will explore more advanced concepts such as navigation, handling user input, and fetching data from APIs.

CHAPTER 5

STYLING IN REACT NATIVE

In React Native, styling plays a crucial role in making apps visually appealing and ensuring a smooth user experience. Unlike traditional web development, React Native doesn't use CSS. Instead, it uses a **JavaScript object-based styling system** that is similar to inline styles in web development, but with some unique nuances specific to mobile platforms.

In this chapter, we will dive into the different ways you can style your React Native components, focusing on the following:

- Inline styles vs. **StyleSheet.create**
- Using **Flexbox** for layout
- Incorporating **third-party libraries** for advanced styling
- A real-world example of styling a **mobile profile page** with Flexbox

---

Inline Styles vs. StyleSheet.create

1. Inline Styles

Inline styles in React Native are JavaScript objects that define the styling properties for components directly within the component itself. You pass the style object to a component via the `style` prop.

Example: Inline Styles

```javascript
import React from 'react';
import { View, Text } from 'react-native';

const InlineStyleExample = () => {
  return (
    <View style={{ flex: 1, justifyContent: 'center', alignItems: 'center', backgroundColor: '#e0e0e0' }}>
      <Text style={{ fontSize: 20, color: '#333' }}>Hello, React Native!</Text>
    </View>
  );
};

export default InlineStyleExample;
```

- **Explanation**:
  - The styles for both the `View` and `Text` components are written directly within the `style` prop as inline JavaScript objects.
  - Inline styles are useful for quick one-off styles, but they have a few drawbacks, such as lack of

reusability and difficulty in managing complex style sheets.

2. StyleSheet.create

`StyleSheet.create` is the recommended approach for styling in React Native. It allows you to define styles separately from the component logic, improving code readability and performance. Using `StyleSheet.create` also helps React Native optimize and pre-process styles.

Example: Using `StyleSheet.create`

javascript

```javascript
import React from 'react';
import { View, Text, StyleSheet } from 'react-native';

const StyleSheetExample = () => {
  return (
    <View style={styles.container}>
      <Text style={styles.text}>Hello, React
Native with StyleSheet!</Text>
    </View>
  );
};

const styles = StyleSheet.create({
```

61

```
container: {
  flex: 1,
  justifyContent: 'center',
  alignItems: 'center',
  backgroundColor: '#f5f5f5',
},
text: {
  fontSize: 18,
  color: '#333',
},
});

export default StyleSheetExample;
```

- **Explanation**:
  - o The styles are defined using `StyleSheet.create`, which provides a clear separation of concerns, making the code cleaner and more maintainable.
  - o By using `StyleSheet.create`, React Native optimizes the processing of styles, resulting in better performance in larger applications.

Why Use `StyleSheet.create`?

- **Performance**: React Native can optimize the styles and ensure that they are only processed once during app rendering, instead of reprocessing them every time the component re-renders.

- **Code organization**: Styles are more structured and can be easily reused across different components.
- **Consistency**: By defining styles separately, you ensure a consistent approach to styling throughout your app.

Flexbox for Layout in React Native

Flexbox is a powerful layout model used in React Native to create complex and responsive layouts. It allows you to align and distribute space among elements within a container, even when their size is unknown or dynamic.

React Native uses a simplified version of Flexbox, but the basic principles are the same as on the web. Here's a brief breakdown of the key Flexbox properties and how they are used in React Native:

Key Flexbox Properties:

1. **flexDirection**: Defines the main axis for layout (horizontal or vertical).
    - o   row: Lays out children horizontally (default).
    - o   column: Lays out children vertically.

2. **justifyContent**: Aligns children along the main axis (horizontal for `row`, vertical for `column`).

   o `flex-start`: Aligns items at the start of the container.

   o `center`: Aligns items in the center.

   o `flex-end`: Aligns items at the end of the container.

   o `space-between`: Distributes items evenly with space between.

   o `space-around`: Distributes items evenly with space around them.

3. **alignItems**: Aligns children along the cross-axis (perpendicular to the main axis).

   o `flex-start`: Aligns items at the start of the container.

   o `center`: Aligns items in the center.

   o `flex-end`: Aligns items at the end of the container.

   o `stretch`: Stretches items to fill the container (default).

4. **flex**: Specifies how a component should grow relative to other components in the container.

Example: Flexbox Layout

javascript

```
import React from 'react';
import { View, Text, StyleSheet } from 'react-
native';

const FlexboxExample = () => {
  return (
    <View style={styles.container}>
      <Text style={styles.box}>Box 1</Text>
      <Text style={styles.box}>Box 2</Text>
      <Text style={styles.box}>Box 3</Text>
    </View>
  );
};

const styles = StyleSheet.create({
  container: {
    flex: 1,
    flexDirection: 'row', // Arrange items
horizontally
    justifyContent: 'space-around', // Space out
boxes evenly
    alignItems: 'center', // Align items in the
center of the cross axis
    backgroundColor: '#f5f5f5',
  },
  box: {
    width: 60,
    height: 60,
    backgroundColor: '#3498db',
```

```
      justifyContent: 'center',
      alignItems: 'center',
      color: 'white',
      textAlign: 'center',
      padding: 10,
   },
});
```

```
export default FlexboxExample;
```

- **Explanation**:
    - o The `container` style uses `flexDirection: 'row'` to lay out the boxes horizontally.
    - o `justifyContent: 'space-around'` spaces the boxes evenly across the main axis.
    - o `alignItems: 'center'` centers the boxes along the cross-axis (vertically).
    - o The result is three boxes spaced evenly across the screen with the text inside aligned in the center.

Using Third-Party Libraries for Styling

While React Native provides built-in tools for styling components, third-party libraries can significantly enhance your development experience by providing additional UI components, theming support, or advanced layouts.

Popular Styling Libraries for React Native:

1. **NativeBase**:
   - o NativeBase is a popular UI library for React Native that provides a set of ready-to-use, customizable components such as buttons, cards, lists, and more.
   - o **Installation**: `npm install native-base`
   - o **Usage**: You can quickly build beautiful UIs with pre-styled components while maintaining customization options.

2. **React Native Paper**:
   - o React Native Paper is another UI library that follows Google's Material Design principles, offering a wide range of components like buttons, dialogs, text inputs, and cards.
   - o **Installation**: `npm install react-native-paper`
   - o **Usage**: React Native Paper provides consistent, responsive, and easily customizable Material Design components.

3. **Styled Components**:
   - o Styled Components allows you to write component-level styles in JavaScript. This CSS-in-JS library is a great way to style your components dynamically and with scoped styles.

- o **Installation**: npm install styled-components
- o **Usage**: It allows you to define styles directly inside the component, leveraging JavaScript for more dynamic styling.

4. **Tailwind CSS for React Native**:
   - o Tailwind CSS, a utility-first CSS framework for the web, has been ported to React Native to provide utility-based styling directly in JSX.
   - o **Installation**: npm install tailwind-rn
   - o **Usage**: Use pre-defined utility classes in your components to manage padding, margin, colors, and layout.

Real-World Example: Styling a Mobile Profile Page with Flexbox

Let's build a **Profile Page** for a mobile app using Flexbox layout. This example will include a profile picture, name, and a short bio, all styled with Flexbox and simple styles.

Example: Profile Page UI with Flexbox

```javascript
import React from 'react';
import { View, Text, Image, StyleSheet } from 'react-native';
```

```
const Profile = () => {
  return (
    <View style={styles.container}>
      <Image
        source={{                          uri:
'https://placekitten.com/200/200' }}
        style={styles.profileImage}
      />
      <Text style={styles.name}>John Doe</Text>
      <Text    style={styles.bio}>A    passionate
mobile developer from San Francisco.</Text>
    </View>
  );
};


const styles = StyleSheet.create({
  container: {
    flex: 1,
    justifyContent: 'center',
    alignItems: 'center',
    backgroundColor: '#f0f0f0',
    padding: 20,
  },
  profileImage: {
    width: 120,
    height: 120,
    borderRadius: 60,
    marginBottom: 20,
```

```
  },
  name: {
    fontSize: 24,
    fontWeight: 'bold',
    marginBottom: 10,
  },
  bio: {
    fontSize: 16,
    color: '#555',
    textAlign: 'center',
    paddingHorizontal: 20,
  },
});

export default Profile;
```

- **Explanation**:
  - The **container** uses Flexbox to center the content horizontally and vertically.
  - The **profileImage** is a circular image (using borderRadius to make it round).
  - The **name** and **bio** texts are styled with fontSize, fontWeight, and other properties to ensure a clean, readable layout.

70

Conclusion

In this chapter, we explored how to style React Native components using inline styles and `StyleSheet.create`. We learned how **Flexbox** helps you create flexible and responsive layouts, and we saw how third-party libraries can improve and speed up your styling workflow.

By mastering styling in React Native, you can create visually appealing, user-friendly mobile applications that work well across both iOS and Android. In the next chapters, we will delve deeper into how to handle user input, navigation, and integrating APIs into your React Native apps.

CHAPTER 6

MANAGING STATE IN REACT NATIVE

In this chapter, we will explore the concept of **state** and **props** in React Native and how they are used to manage and pass data between components. Managing state is one of the core aspects of building dynamic and interactive applications, and we will dive into **React hooks** such as useState and useEffect to handle state management in functional components.

Additionally, we will build a real-world example: a **counter app** that demonstrates state management in action.

Understanding State and Props in React Native

State in React Native

- **State** is used to store data that changes over time and needs to be reflected in the UI. It's local to a component and can be updated through user interactions or network responses.
- Whenever the state changes, React triggers a re-render of the component to reflect the updated state in the UI.

- In React Native, state is typically used to track things like user input, app settings, or any other data that will change during the app's lifecycle.

Example: Setting up state

javascript

```javascript
import React, { useState } from 'react';
import { View, Text, Button } from 'react-native';

const Counter = () => {
  const [count, setCount] = useState(0);   // Initializing state

  return (
    <View>
      <Text>Count: {count}</Text>
      <Button title="Increment" onPress={() => setCount(count + 1)} />
    </View>
  );
};

export default Counter;
```

- In this example, `useState(0)` initializes the state variable `count` to 0, and `setCount` is used to update the state when the button is pressed.

Props in React Native

- **Props** (short for "properties") are used to pass data from one component to another. They are read-only and allow you to pass data from a parent component to its child components.
- Props are immutable within the child component, meaning the child cannot modify the props directly.

Example: Passing data through props

javascript

```
import React from 'react';
import { View, Text } from 'react-native';

const Greeting = ({ name }) => {
  return <Text>Hello, {name}!</Text>;
};

const Parent = () => {
  return (
    <View>
      <Greeting name="John" />
      <Greeting name="Jane" />
```

```
    </View>
  );
};
```

```
export default Parent;
```

- In this example, the Greeting component receives a prop called name and renders a greeting message based on that prop. The Parent component passes different values for name to each Greeting component.

Using Hooks Like useState and useEffect for State Management

1. useState Hook

useState is a React hook that allows you to add state to functional components. It returns an array with two elements:

1. The current state value
2. A function to update the state

Example: Counter with useState

```
javascript
```

```
import React, { useState } from 'react';
```

```
import { View, Text, Button } from 'react-
native';

const Counter = () => {
  const [count, setCount] = useState(0);   //
State with initial value of 0

  const increment = () => setCount(count + 1);
  const decrement = () => setCount(count - 1);

  return (
    <View>
      <Text>Count: {count}</Text>
      <Button                title="Increment"
onPress={increment} />
      <Button                title="Decrement"
onPress={decrement} />
    </View>
  );
};

export default Counter;
```

- useState(0) initializes the count variable at 0.
- The increment and decrement functions modify the state by calling setCount.

2. useEffect Hook

useEffect is another React hook that lets you run side effects in functional components, such as data fetching, subscriptions, or manually changing the DOM. useEffect is called after the render and can be used to perform operations like fetching data or setting up event listeners.

- By default, useEffect runs after every render, but you can control when it runs by passing a dependency array.

Example: Using useEffect for fetching data

javascript

```
import React, { useState, useEffect } from
'react';
import { View, Text, Button } from 'react-
native';

const FetchData = () => {
  const [data, setData] = useState(null);

  useEffect(() => {

fetch('https://jsonplaceholder.typicode.com/pos
ts/1')
      .then(response => response.json())
      .then(json => setData(json))
```

77

```
      .catch(error => console.error(error));
  }, []);  // Empty array means this effect runs
only once after the first render

  return (
    <View>
      {data ? (
        <Text>{data.title}</Text>
      ) : (
        <Text>Loading...</Text>
      )}
    </View>
  );
};

export default FetchData;
```

- The useEffect hook is used here to fetch data from an API after the component mounts (initial render). The empty array [] ensures that the effect only runs once when the component is first loaded.

Passing Data Through Props and State Management Across Components

State is often passed down to child components through props. Managing state across multiple components can be done by lifting state up to a common ancestor or using a global state management tool like **Redux**. However, in smaller apps, passing state through props and lifting it up is usually sufficient.

Example: Lifting State Up

If you have multiple components that need to share state, you can lift the state up to their nearest common ancestor and pass it down via props.

```javascript
import React, { useState } from 'react';
import { View, Text, Button } from 'react-native';

const CounterDisplay = ({ count }) => {
  return <Text>Count: {count}</Text>;
};

const CounterControls = ({ increment, decrement }) => {
  return (
    <View>
      <Button                 title="Increment"
onPress={increment} />
      <Button                 title="Decrement"
onPress={decrement} />
    </View>
  );
```

```
};

const CounterApp = () => {
  const [count, setCount] = useState(0);

  const increment = () => setCount(count + 1);
  const decrement = () => setCount(count - 1);

  return (
    <View>
      <CounterDisplay count={count} />
      <CounterControls    increment={increment}
decrement={decrement} />
    </View>
  );
};

export default CounterApp;
```

- **Explanation**:
  - The `CounterApp` component manages the `count` state.
  - `CounterDisplay` and `CounterControls` are both child components that receive state and functions as props.
  - This is a simple example of **lifting state up**: the parent component (`CounterApp`) manages the state, and the child components

80

(CounterDisplay and CounterControls) receive the state and update functions as props.

Real-World Example: Building a Counter App with State Management

Let's build a **Counter App** where the user can increment and decrement a counter, and the app will display the updated count. This will demonstrate how to use **state**, **props**, and **hooks** in a practical application.

javascript

```javascript
import React, { useState } from 'react';
import { View, Text, Button, StyleSheet } from
'react-native';

const CounterApp = () => {
  const [count, setCount] = useState(0);    //
Manage the counter state

  const increment = () => setCount(count + 1);
// Increment the counter
  const decrement = () => setCount(count - 1);
// Decrement the counter

  return (
    <View style={styles.container}>
```

```
      <Text            style={styles.text}>Counter:
{count}</Text>
      <View style={styles.buttonContainer}>
        <Button                  title="Increment"
onPress={increment} />
        <Button                  title="Decrement"
onPress={decrement} />
      </View>
    </View>
  );
};


const styles = StyleSheet.create({
  container: {
    flex: 1,
    justifyContent: 'center',
    alignItems: 'center',
    backgroundColor: '#fff',
  },
  text: {
    fontSize: 30,
    marginBottom: 20,
  },
  buttonContainer: {
    flexDirection: 'row',
    justifyContent: 'space-between',
    width: 200,
  },
});
```

```
export default CounterApp;
```

- **Explanation**:
  - o The `CounterApp` component uses the `useState` hook to manage the `count` state.
  - o The `increment` and `decrement` functions update the state when the corresponding buttons are pressed.
  - o The app layout uses **Flexbox** for arranging the buttons horizontally.

Conclusion

In this chapter, we've covered the fundamental concepts of **state** and **props** in React Native, which are essential for building dynamic, interactive applications. We explored how to use the `useState` and `useEffect` hooks to manage state and side effects in functional components. Additionally, we demonstrated how state can be passed down through props and how to lift state up to parent components for sharing across child components.

By mastering state management and props, you can build powerful React Native apps that respond to user interactions and dynamically update the UI. In the following chapters, we'll delve into more advanced concepts, including handling user input, navigation, and data fetching.

CHAPTER 7

NAVIGATION IN REACT NATIVE

In mobile development, navigation is essential for moving between different screens and sections of your app. In React Native, **React Navigation** is the most commonly used library for implementing navigation in mobile apps. In this chapter, we'll explore the basics of **React Navigation**, including different navigation patterns such as **stack**, **tab**, and **drawer navigation**. We'll also cover how to navigate between screens and pass parameters to manage data flow between different parts of your app.

Introduction to React Navigation

React Navigation is a flexible and powerful navigation library for React Native. It allows you to manage different types of navigation patterns in your app, making it easy to switch between screens, pass data, and organize your app's structure.

To use React Navigation, you need to install the core navigation package as well as other dependencies for different types of navigation.

85

Installing React Navigation

To start using React Navigation, follow these steps:

1. Install the core `react-navigation` package:

   bash

   ```
   npm install @react-navigation/native
   ```

2. Install the required dependencies:

   bash

   ```
   npm install react-native-screens react-native-safe-area-context
   ```

3. For **stack** navigation, install the `react-navigation-stack` package:

   bash

   ```
   npm install @react-navigation/stack
   ```

4. For **tab** navigation, install the `react-navigation-tabs` package:

   bash

   ```
   npm install @react-navigation/bottom-tabs
   ```

5. For **drawer** navigation, install the `react-navigation-drawer` package:

```bash
```

```
npm install @react-navigation/drawer
```

Once you have installed the necessary packages, you can set up and use navigation in your app.

Stack, Tab, and Drawer Navigation

React Navigation offers different types of navigation patterns. Let's explore three of the most commonly used ones: **Stack Navigation**, **Tab Navigation**, and **Drawer Navigation**.

1. Stack Navigation

Stack Navigation allows you to push and pop screens on a stack, making it easy to create a "screen stack" for navigating between screens in a linear way. This is typically used for navigating between different pages or views in an app, where you go from one screen to the next and can return to previous screens.

Example: Stack Navigation

```javascript
```

87

```
import * as React from 'react';
import { Button, View, Text } from 'react-
native';
import { NavigationContainer } from '@react-
navigation/native';
import { createStackNavigator } from '@react-
navigation/stack';

const HomeScreen = ({ navigation }) => {
  return (
    <View>
      <Text>Home Screen</Text>
      <Button title="Go to Details" onPress={()
=> navigation.navigate('Details')} />
    </View>
  );
};

const DetailsScreen = () => {
  return (
    <View>
      <Text>Details Screen</Text>
    </View>
  );
};

const Stack = createStackNavigator();

const App = () => {
```

```
    return (
      <NavigationContainer>
        <Stack.Navigator>
          <Stack.Screen            name="Home"
component={HomeScreen} />
          <Stack.Screen            name="Details"
component={DetailsScreen} />
        </Stack.Navigator>
      </NavigationContainer>
    );
};

export default App;
```

- **Explanation**:
  - o   HomeScreen contains a button that navigates to the DetailsScreen.
  - o   The createStackNavigator function is used to define the stack navigation and declare the screens.
  - o   navigation.navigate('Details') triggers the transition to the Details screen.

2. Tab Navigation

Tab Navigation is commonly used for apps that require a set of main navigation options, where each option is displayed as a tab.

Typically, tabs are used for main sections of the app, like the home page, search, profile, or settings.

Example: Tab Navigation

javascript

```
import * as React from 'react';
import { createBottomTabNavigator } from '@react-
navigation/bottom-tabs';
import { NavigationContainer } from '@react-
navigation/native';
import { View, Text } from 'react-native';

const HomeScreen = () => {
  return (
    <View>
      <Text>Home Screen</Text>
    </View>
  );
};

const SettingsScreen = () => {
  return (
    <View>
      <Text>Settings Screen</Text>
    </View>
  );
};
```

```
const Tab = createBottomTabNavigator();

const App = () => {
  return (
    <NavigationContainer>
      <Tab.Navigator>
        <Tab.Screen                name="Home"
component={HomeScreen} />
        <Tab.Screen                name="Settings"
component={SettingsScreen} />
      </Tab.Navigator>
    </NavigationContainer>
  );
};

export default App;
```

- **Explanation**:
  - o The createBottomTabNavigator function is used to create the bottom tabs. You define which screens should appear as tabs, and the tab navigator handles switching between them.
  - o HomeScreen and SettingsScreen are the two tabs that users can navigate between.

3. Drawer Navigation

Drawer Navigation provides a way to navigate the app via a side menu that can be pulled out from the left or right side of the screen. This is commonly used for apps with a lot of sections, like social media apps or e-commerce platforms.

Example: Drawer Navigation

javascript

```javascript
import * as React from 'react';
import { createDrawerNavigator } from '@react-
navigation/drawer';
import { NavigationContainer } from '@react-
navigation/native';
import { View, Text } from 'react-native';

const HomeScreen = () => {
  return (
    <View>
      <Text>Home Screen</Text>
    </View>
  );
};

const ProfileScreen = () => {
  return (
    <View>
```

```
      <Text>Profile Screen</Text>
    </View>
  );
};


const Drawer = createDrawerNavigator();

const App = () => {
  return (
    <NavigationContainer>
      <Drawer.Navigator>
        <Drawer.Screen              name="Home"
component={HomeScreen} />
        <Drawer.Screen              name="Profile"
component={ProfileScreen} />
      </Drawer.Navigator>
    </NavigationContainer>
  );
};

export default App;
```

- **Explanation**:
  - o The createDrawerNavigator function is used to create a side drawer. It defines the sections of your app that will be available in the drawer.
  - o Users can swipe or tap the menu icon to open the drawer and navigate between HomeScreen and ProfileScreen.

93

Navigating Between Screens and Passing Parameters

One of the key features of React Navigation is the ability to navigate between screens and pass parameters to them. This enables you to send data between different parts of your app.

Navigating Between Screens with Parameters

To pass parameters to a screen, you use the `navigation.navigate` method and include the parameters in the second argument as an object.

Example: Passing Parameters Between Screens

```javascript
import * as React from 'react';
import { Button, View, Text } from 'react-native';
import { NavigationContainer } from '@react-navigation/native';
import { createStackNavigator } from '@react-navigation/stack';

const HomeScreen = ({ navigation }) => {
  return (
    <View>
      <Text>Home Screen</Text>
```

94

```
    <Button
      title="Go to Details"
      onPress={()                              =>
navigation.navigate('Details',   {   itemId:   42,
otherParam: 'anything' })}
      />
    </View>
  );
};


const DetailsScreen = ({ route }) => {
  const { itemId, otherParam } = route.params;
  return (
    <View>
      <Text>Details Screen</Text>
      <Text>Item ID: {itemId}</Text>
      <Text>Other Param: {otherParam}</Text>
    </View>
  );
};


const Stack = createStackNavigator();

const App = () => {
  return (
    <NavigationContainer>
      <Stack.Navigator>
        <Stack.Screen                    name="Home"
component={HomeScreen} />
```

```
      <Stack.Screen              name="Details"
component={DetailsScreen} />
      </Stack.Navigator>
    </NavigationContainer>
  );
};

export default App;
```

- **Explanation**:
  - o In the `HomeScreen`, when the button is pressed, we use `navigation.navigate('Details', { itemId: 42, otherParam: 'anything' })` to pass `itemId` and `otherParam` as parameters to the `DetailsScreen`.
  - o In the `DetailsScreen`, we use `route.params` to access the parameters that were passed.

Real-World Example: Creating a Simple App with Multiple Screens Using Navigation

Let's build a simple app with multiple screens: **Home**, **Details**, and **Profile**. We will use **stack navigation** to move between screens, **pass parameters** to the details screen, and create a navigation structure for a user profile.

Example: Simple Multi-Screen App

```javascript

import * as React from 'react';
import { View, Text, Button } from 'react-native';
import { NavigationContainer } from '@react-navigation/native';
import { createStackNavigator } from '@react-navigation/stack';

const HomeScreen = ({ navigation }) => {
  return (
    <View>
      <Text>Home Screen</Text>
      <Button
        title="Go to Details"
        onPress={()                       => navigation.navigate('Details', { itemId: 1 })}
      />
      <Button
        title="Go to Profile"
        onPress={()                        => navigation.navigate('Profile')}
      />
    </View>
  );
};

const DetailsScreen = ({ route }) => {
```

97

```
  const { itemId } = route.params;
  return (
    <View>
      <Text>Details Screen</Text>
      <Text>Item ID: {itemId}</Text>
    </View>
  );
};


const ProfileScreen = () => {
  return (
    <View>
      <Text>Profile Screen</Text>
    </View>
  );
};


const Stack = createStackNavigator();

const App = () => {
  return (
    <NavigationContainer>
      <Stack.Navigator>
        <Stack.Screen               name="Home"
component={HomeScreen} />
        <Stack.Screen             name="Details"
component={DetailsScreen} />
        <Stack.Screen             name="Profile"
component={ProfileScreen} />
```

```
        </Stack.Navigator>
      </NavigationContainer>
  );
};

export default App;
```

- **Explanation**:
  - o The app has three screens: Home, Details, and Profile.
  - o We use **stack navigation** to navigate between the screens.
  - o On the **Home** screen, we have buttons that navigate to the Details and Profile screens, passing parameters to Details (in this case, itemId).

Conclusion

In this chapter, we've learned how to implement navigation in React Native using **React Navigation**. We covered different types of navigation patterns: **stack**, **tab**, and **drawer navigation**, and explored how to navigate between screens and pass parameters. By using React Navigation, you can easily manage transitions between screens and provide a smooth user experience in your app.

In the next chapters, we'll explore more advanced topics, including state management, handling user input, and integrating external data through APIs.

Part 3

Intermediate Concepts in React Native

CHAPTER 8

HANDLING USER INPUT AND FORMS

In this chapter, we'll dive into how to handle various types of user input in React Native, such as text input, checkboxes, and buttons. We'll also look at how to manage form state, perform validation, and create interactive forms. Building forms with proper validation is essential in most mobile apps, from sign-up forms to contact forms, and we'll explore the most common practices for creating robust and user-friendly forms.

Handling Text Input, Checkboxes, and Buttons

1. Handling Text Input

The `TextInput` component is used to capture user input in React Native. This component allows users to type text into the app, such as in a search box, login form, or sign-up form. You can manage the state of the `TextInput` component by using the `value` and `onChangeText` props.

Example: Basic TextInput

```javascript
```

```
import React, { useState } from 'react';
import { View, TextInput, Text, StyleSheet } from
'react-native';

const TextInputExample = () => {
  const [text, setText] = useState('');

  return (
    <View style={styles.container}>
      <TextInput
        style={styles.input}
        placeholder="Enter some text"
        value={text}
        onChangeText={setText}
      />
      <Text>You typed: {text}</Text>
    </View>
  );
};

const styles = StyleSheet.create({
  container: {
    flex: 1,
    justifyContent: 'center',
    alignItems: 'center',
  },
  input: {
    height: 40,
```

```
    borderColor: 'gray',
    borderWidth: 1,
    width: '80%',
    marginBottom: 20,
    paddingLeft: 10,
  },
});
```

```
export default TextInputExample;
```

- **Explanation**:
  - o   TextInput is used to create a field where the user can input text.
  - o   The value prop binds the input field to the text state, while the onChangeText prop updates the state whenever the user types.
  - o   As the user types, the text state is updated and reflected in the displayed text below the input field.

2. Handling Checkboxes

For handling boolean user input (such as a checkbox), React Native provides the Switch and CheckBox components. The Switch component is commonly used for on/off states, while CheckBox is used for selection.

Example: Using Switch for Boolean Input

104

```javascript

import React, { useState } from 'react';
import { View, Switch, Text, StyleSheet } from
'react-native';

const SwitchExample = () => {
  const [isEnabled, setIsEnabled] =
useState(false);

  const toggleSwitch = () =>
setIsEnabled(previousState => !previousState);

  return (
    <View style={styles.container}>
      <Text>{isEnabled ? "Switch is ON" : "Switch
is OFF"}</Text>
      <Switch
        value={isEnabled}
        onValueChange={toggleSwitch}
      />
    </View>
  );
};

const styles = StyleSheet.create({
  container: {
    flex: 1,
    justifyContent: 'center',
```

105

```
    alignItems: 'center',
  },
});
```

```
export default SwitchExample;
```

- **Explanation**:
  - o The `Switch` component is used to toggle the value of `isEnabled`, and the state changes when the user interacts with the switch.
  - o The `onValueChange` handler updates the state (`isEnabled`) each time the switch is toggled.

3. Handling Buttons

Buttons are used to trigger actions in React Native. The `Button` component is used for simple button implementations, and it provides an `onPress` prop to handle the click or tap event.

Example: Using a Button to Handle Actions

javascript

```
import React from 'react';
import { View, Button, Alert, StyleSheet } from
'react-native';

const ButtonExample = () => {
  const showAlert = () => {
```

```
    Alert.alert('Button Pressed', 'You pressed
the button!');
  };

  return (
    <View style={styles.container}>
      <Button          title="Press          Me"
onPress={showAlert} />
    </View>
  );
};

const styles = StyleSheet.create({
  container: {
    flex: 1,
    justifyContent: 'center',
    alignItems: 'center',
  },
});

export default ButtonExample;
```

- **Explanation**:
  - o The Button component displays a button with the title "Press Me".
  - o When the button is pressed, the showAlert function is called, displaying a simple alert message.

107

Managing Form State and Validation

Forms often require managing multiple pieces of data and performing validation. State is used to track the values entered by the user, and you can apply validation logic to ensure that the input meets certain criteria (e.g., email format, password strength).

1. Managing Form State

You can use the `useState` hook to manage multiple form fields. In a complex form, you might use multiple `useState` hooks to manage different fields (e.g., username, email, password). For simpler forms, you can combine them into a single state object.

Example: Managing Form State

javascript

```
import React, { useState } from 'react';
import { View, TextInput, Button, Text,
StyleSheet } from 'react-native';

const SignUpForm = () => {
  const [formData, setFormData] = useState({
    username: '',
    email: '',
    password: ''
  });
```

```
const handleInputChange = (field, value) => {
  setFormData({
    ...formData,
    [field]: value
  });
};

const handleSubmit = () => {
  // Form submission logic
  console.log(formData);
};

return (
  <View style={styles.container}>
    <TextInput
      style={styles.input}
      placeholder="Username"
      value={formData.username}
      onChangeText={text                 =>
handleInputChange('username', text)}
    />
    <TextInput
      style={styles.input}
      placeholder="Email"
      value={formData.email}
      onChangeText={text                 =>
handleInputChange('email', text)}
    />
```

```
      <TextInput
        style={styles.input}
        placeholder="Password"
        secureTextEntry
        value={formData.password}
        onChangeText={text                   =>
handleInputChange('password', text)}
      />
      <Button           title="Sign           Up"
onPress={handleSubmit} />
    </View>
  );
};

const styles = StyleSheet.create({
  container: {
    flex: 1,
    justifyContent: 'center',
    alignItems: 'center',
    padding: 20,
  },
  input: {
    height: 40,
    borderColor: 'gray',
    borderWidth: 1,
    marginBottom: 10,
    paddingLeft: 10,
    width: '100%',
  },
```

```
});
```

```
export default SignUpForm;
```

- **Explanation**:
  - o `formData` is an object containing `username`, `email`, and `password`.
  - o `handleInputChange` updates the specific field value in `formData` when the user types into the `TextInput` fields.
  - o The `handleSubmit` function logs the form data when the "Sign Up" button is pressed.

2. Form Validation

Validation ensures that the user has entered valid data before submitting the form. For example, you may want to check that the email is in the correct format or that the password meets certain requirements.

Example: Simple Form Validation

javascript

```
import React, { useState } from 'react';
import { View, TextInput, Button, Text,
StyleSheet, Alert } from 'react-native';
```

```
const SignUpForm = () => {
  const [formData, setFormData] = useState({
    username: '',
    email: '',
    password: ''
  });

  const handleInputChange = (field, value) => {
    setFormData({
      ...formData,
      [field]: value
    });
  };

  const validateForm = () => {
    const { username, email, password } =
formData;
    if (!username || !email || !password) {
      Alert.alert('Error',   'All   fields   are
required');
      return false;
    }
    const           emailPattern              =
/^[^\s@]+@[^\s@]+\.[^\s@]+$/;
    if (!emailPattern.test(email)) {
      Alert.alert('Error',    'Invalid    email
format');
      return false;
    }
```

```
    if (password.length < 6) {
       Alert.alert('Error', 'Password must be at
least 6 characters');
       return false;
    }
    return true;
  };


  const handleSubmit = () => {
    if (validateForm()) {
       Alert.alert('Success',        'Sign        Up
Successful');
       console.log(formData);
    }
  };


  return (
    <View style={styles.container}>
      <TextInput
        style={styles.input}
        placeholder="Username"
        value={formData.username}
        onChangeText={text                    =>
handleInputChange('username', text)}
      />
      <TextInput
        style={styles.input}
        placeholder="Email"
        value={formData.email}
```

```
        onChangeText={text                    =>
handleInputChange('email', text)}
      />
      <TextInput
        style={styles.input}
        placeholder="Password"
        secureTextEntry
        value={formData.password}
        onChangeText={text                    =>
handleInputChange('password', text)}
      />
      <Button            title="Sign        Up"
onPress={handleSubmit} />
    </View>
  );
};

const styles = StyleSheet.create({
  container: {
    flex: 1,
    justifyContent: 'center',
    alignItems: 'center',
    padding: 20,
  },
  input: {
    height: 40,
    borderColor: 'gray',
    borderWidth: 1,
    marginBottom: 10,
```

```
    paddingLeft: 10,
    width: '100%',
  },
});
```

```
export default SignUpForm;
```

- **Explanation**:
  - o `validateForm` checks if all fields are filled and if the email and password meet the necessary criteria.
  - o If the form is invalid, an `Alert` is shown. If the form is valid, the data is logged and a success message is shown.

Conclusion

In this chapter, we learned how to handle user input in React Native using components like `TextInput`, `Switch`, and `Button`. We also explored how to manage form state using the `useState` hook and how to perform **form validation** to ensure that users provide the correct input. We also saw a real-world example of creating a sign-up form with validation.

Handling forms and user input is a common task in mobile app development, and by using the techniques covered in this chapter, you can create user-friendly forms that ensure data integrity and enhance the user experience. In the following chapters, we will dive into more advanced topics like navigation, data handling, and API integration.

CHAPTER 9

WORKING WITH APIS IN REACT NATIVE

In modern mobile applications, interacting with external data sources is essential. Whether it's fetching user data, displaying news articles, or integrating third-party services, **APIs (Application Programming Interfaces)** allow your app to retrieve and interact with data over the internet.

In this chapter, we will explore how to fetch data from APIs using two popular methods: `fetch` and `axios`. You'll also learn how to display fetched data within React Native components. Finally, we will build a simple **weather app** that pulls data from a public API, providing a real-world example of how to work with APIs in React Native.

Fetching Data from APIs Using `fetch` *and* `axios`

1. Using `fetch` to Retrieve Data

`fetch` is a built-in JavaScript function for making HTTP requests. It's part of the standard JavaScript API, so you don't need to install any additional libraries to use it. It returns a **Promise** that resolves to the response of the request.

Basic Syntax of `fetch`:

```javascript
fetch(url, options)
  .then(response => response.json())   // Parse JSON response
  .then(data => console.log(data))     // Handle the data
  .catch(error => console.error(error));   // Handle any errors
```

Example: Fetching Data Using `fetch`

```javascript
import React, { useState, useEffect } from 'react';
import { View, Text, StyleSheet } from 'react-native';

const FetchExample = () => {
  const [data, setData] = useState(null);
  const [loading, setLoading] = useState(true);
  const [error, setError] = useState(null);

  useEffect(() => {
```

```
fetch('https://api.openweathermap.org/data/2.5/
weather?q=London&appid=YOUR_API_KEY')
      .then(response => response.json())
      .then(data => {
        setData(data);
        setLoading(false);
      })
      .catch(error => {
        setError(error);
        setLoading(false);
      });
  }, []);

  if (loading) {
    return <Text>Loading...</Text>;
  }

  if (error) {
    return <Text>Error: {error.message}</Text>;
  }

  return (
    <View style={styles.container}>
      <Text>Weather in {data.name}</Text>
      <Text>Temperature:
{data.main.temp}°C</Text>
      <Text>Condition:
{data.weather[0].description}</Text>
```

```
    </View>
  );
};


const styles = StyleSheet.create({
  container: {
    flex: 1,
    justifyContent: 'center',
    alignItems: 'center',
  },
});


export default FetchExample;
```

- **Explanation**:
    - `fetch` retrieves weather data for London from OpenWeather API.
    - The `useEffect` hook fetches the data when the component mounts.
    - Once the data is fetched, it updates the state (`data`) and stops the loading indicator (`loading`).

2. Using `axios` to Retrieve Data

`axios` is a promise-based HTTP client for the browser and Node.js. It provides a more powerful and flexible API compared to `fetch`, and it's often preferred for more complex requests.

Installation:

```bash
npm install axios
```

Basic Syntax of axios:

```javascript
import axios from 'axios';

axios.get(url, { headers })
  .then(response => console.log(response.data))
// Handle response data
  .catch(error => console.error(error));    //
Handle errors
```

Example: Fetching Data Using axios

```javascript
import React, { useState, useEffect } from
'react';
import { View, Text, StyleSheet } from 'react-
native';
import axios from 'axios';

const AxiosExample = () => {
  const [data, setData] = useState(null);
```

121

```
const [loading, setLoading] = useState(true);
const [error, setError] = useState(null);

useEffect(() => {
  axios

.get('https://api.openweathermap.org/data/2.5/w
eather?q=London&appid=YOUR_API_KEY')
      .then(response => {
        setData(response.data);
        setLoading(false);
      })
      .catch(error => {
        setError(error);
        setLoading(false);
      });
}, []);

if (loading) {
  return <Text>Loading...</Text>;
}

if (error) {
  return <Text>Error: {error.message}</Text>;
}

return (
  <View style={styles.container}>
    <Text>Weather in {data.name}</Text>
```

```
      <Text>Temperature:
{data.main.temp}°C</Text>
      <Text>Condition:
{data.weather[0].description}</Text>
    </View>
  );
};


const styles = StyleSheet.create({
  container: {
    flex: 1,
    justifyContent: 'center',
    alignItems: 'center',
  },
});


export default AxiosExample;
```

- **Explanation**:
  - o   axios is used to fetch the weather data.
  - o   Similar to fetch, the useEffect hook is used to perform the request when the component mounts, but axios provides additional features like automatic JSON parsing.

Displaying Fetched Data in React Native Components

Once the data is fetched from the API, it's stored in the component's state (using `useState` in functional components), and you can render it using React Native components such as `Text`, `Image`, or `View`.

- The `Text` component is commonly used to display strings, numbers, or JSON data in a readable format.
- You can also format the data before displaying it. For example, the weather temperature could be converted from Kelvin to Celsius or Fahrenheit.

Real-World Example: Creating a Weather App that Pulls Data from a Public API

Now let's combine everything we've learned to create a simple weather app that retrieves weather data from the **OpenWeather API**. The app will display the current temperature, weather conditions, and location name.

1. Setting Up the App

1. **Sign up for an API Key**:
    o Go to the OpenWeather website and sign up to get an API key that allows you to fetch weather data.

124

2. **Install Dependencies**:

   o   If you're using `axios`, install it via:

```bash
bash
```

```bash
npm install axios
```

3. **Creating the Weather App**:

Example: WeatherApp.js

```javascript
javascript

import React, { useState, useEffect } from
'react';
import { View, Text, TextInput, Button,
StyleSheet, Alert } from 'react-native';
import axios from 'axios';

const WeatherApp = () => {
  const [city, setCity] = useState('');
  const [weather, setWeather] = useState(null);
  const [loading, setLoading] = useState(false);
  const [error, setError] = useState(null);

  const fetchWeather = () => {
    if (!city) {
      Alert.alert('Error', 'Please enter a city
name');
      return;
```

125

```
    }

    setLoading(true);
    setError(null);

    axios

.get(`https://api.openweathermap.org/data/2.5/w
eather?q=${city}&appid=YOUR_API_KEY&units=metri
c`)
      .then(response => {
        setWeather(response.data);
        setLoading(false);
      })
      .catch(error => {
        setError('Failed   to    fetch    weather
data');
        setLoading(false);
      });
  };

  return (
    <View style={styles.container}>
      <Text          style={styles.title}>Weather
App</Text>
      <TextInput
        style={styles.input}
        placeholder="Enter city name"
        value={city}
```

```
        onChangeText={setCity}
      />
      <Button         title="Get        Weather"
onPress={fetchWeather} />

      {loading && <Text>Loading...</Text>}

      {error              &&              <Text
style={styles.error}>{error}</Text>}

      {weather && (
        <View style={styles.weatherContainer}>
          <Text
style={styles.city}>{weather.name}</Text>
          <Text
style={styles.temperature}>{weather.main.temp}°
C</Text>
          <Text
style={styles.condition}>{weather.weather[0].de
scription}</Text>
        </View>
      )}
    </View>
  );
};

const styles = StyleSheet.create({
  container: {
    flex: 1,
```

```
    justifyContent: 'center',
    alignItems: 'center',
    padding: 20,
  },
  title: {
    fontSize: 30,
    fontWeight: 'bold',
    marginBottom: 20,
  },
  input: {
    height: 40,
    borderColor: 'gray',
    borderWidth: 1,
    width: '100%',
    marginBottom: 20,
    paddingLeft: 10,
  },
  weatherContainer: {
    alignItems: 'center',
    marginTop: 20,
  },
  city: {
    fontSize: 24,
    fontWeight: 'bold',
  },
  temperature: {
    fontSize: 40,
    fontWeight: 'bold',
  },
```

```
condition: {
  fontSize: 20,
  color: 'gray',
},
error: {
  color: 'red',
},
});
```

```
export default WeatherApp;
```

- **Explanation**:
  - o **State Management**: We use `useState` to store the city name (`city`), weather data (`weather`), and manage loading and error states.
  - o **Fetching Weather Data**: When the user enters a city and clicks the "Get Weather" button, the `fetchWeather` function is called. It fetches weather data using `axios` from the OpenWeather API.
  - o **Displaying Data**: Once the data is fetched, we display the city name, temperature, and weather condition.
  - o **Handling Errors**: If there's an error (e.g., no city entered or an invalid city), an error message is shown.

Conclusion

In this chapter, we explored how to fetch data from external APIs using both `fetch` and `axios`. We learned how to display the fetched data using React Native components, manage loading and error states, and interact with public APIs like OpenWeather to create a simple weather app.

API integration is crucial for many apps that rely on external data, and React Native provides an easy way to connect your app to the internet and present data to users in a meaningful way. In the next chapters, we'll continue to build on this knowledge and explore how to manage state and implement more complex features like navigation and data persistence.

CHAPTER 10

DATA PERSISTENCE IN REACT NATIVE

In mobile applications, it's often necessary to store data locally, whether for caching, offline functionality, or simply to maintain state across sessions. React Native provides several solutions for data persistence, and in this chapter, we will explore two commonly used methods:

- **AsyncStorage**: A simple key-value storage system for storing small amounts of data.
- **SQLite**: A relational database solution for more complex data storage needs.

By the end of this chapter, we'll create a **to-do app** with local data storage, allowing users to add, edit, and delete tasks, even when the app is offline.

Storing Data Locally with AsyncStorage

AsyncStorage is a simple, asynchronous, persistent, key-value storage system that allows you to store data in the form of strings.

It is ideal for storing small amounts of data like user preferences, session data, or small forms of non-relational data.

Installing AsyncStorage

First, install the required package:

bash

```
npm install @react-native-async-storage/async-storage
```

Basic Usage of AsyncStorage

1. **Storing Data**: Use the `setItem` method to store data.
2. **Retrieving Data**: Use the `getItem` method to retrieve stored data.
3. **Removing Data**: Use the `removeItem` method to delete data.

Example: Storing and Retrieving Data Using AsyncStorage

javascript

```javascript
import React, { useState, useEffect } from 'react';
import { View, Text, Button, StyleSheet } from 'react-native';
import AsyncStorage from '@react-native-async-storage/async-storage';
```

```
const AsyncStorageExample = () => {
  const [value, setValue] = useState(null);

  useEffect(() => {
    // Fetch the stored value when the component
mounts
    AsyncStorage.getItem('name')
      .then(storedValue => {
        if (storedValue) {
          setValue(storedValue);
        }
      })
      .catch(error => console.error(error));
  }, []);

  const storeData = () => {
    // Store a value
    AsyncStorage.setItem('name', 'John Doe')
      .then(() => {
        setValue('John Doe');
      })
      .catch(error => console.error(error));
  };

  const removeData = () => {
    // Remove the value
    AsyncStorage.removeItem('name')
      .then(() => {
```

```
        setValue(null);
      })
      .catch(error => console.error(error));
  };


  return (
    <View style={styles.container}>
      <Text>{value ? `Stored Name: ${value}` :
'No name stored'}</Text>
      <Button        title="Store        Name"
onPress={storeData} />
      <Button        title="Remove        Name"
onPress={removeData} />
    </View>
  );
};


const styles = StyleSheet.create({
  container: {
    flex: 1,
    justifyContent: 'center',
    alignItems: 'center',
  },
});


export default AsyncStorageExample;
```

- **Explanation**:

- o `AsyncStorage.setItem('name', 'John Doe')` stores the name 'John Doe' under the key `'name'`.
- o `AsyncStorage.getItem('name')` retrieves the stored value.
- o `AsyncStorage.removeItem('name')` removes the stored data.

Using SQLite for Offline Data Storage

While `AsyncStorage` is great for small amounts of data, it's not suited for more complex data or relational data storage. For such needs, you can use **SQLite**, which is a lightweight relational database for mobile apps.

Installing SQLite

To use SQLite in React Native, we need to install a third-party library:

```bash
npm install react-native-sqlite-storage
```

Basic Usage of SQLite

1. **Open/Create a Database**: Open or create a database using `openDatabase`.

2. **Create Tables**: Use SQL queries to create tables.

3. **Insert Data**: Insert data into the table using `executeSql`.

4. **Query Data**: Retrieve data using SQL `SELECT` queries.

Example: Basic SQLite Example

```javascript
import React, { useState, useEffect } from 'react';
import { View, Text, Button, StyleSheet } from 'react-native';
import SQLite from 'react-native-sqlite-storage';

const db = SQLite.openDatabase({ name: 'todo.db', location: 'default' });

const SQLiteExample = () => {
  const [tasks, setTasks] = useState([]);

  useEffect(() => {
    db.transaction(txn => {
      txn.executeSql(
        'CREATE TABLE IF NOT EXISTS tasks (id INTEGER PRIMARY KEY AUTOINCREMENT, task TEXT)',
        [],
```

```
        ()      =>    console.log('Table    created
successfully'),
        error  =>  console.log('Error    creating
table', error)
      );
    });
  }, []);

  const addTask = () => {
    db.transaction(txn => {
      txn.executeSql(
        'INSERT INTO tasks (task) VALUES (?)',
        ['New Task'],
        () => {
          console.log('Task added');
          fetchTasks(); // Reload tasks after
adding a new one
        },
        error  =>  console.log('Error    adding
task', error)
      );
    });
  };

  const fetchTasks = () => {
    db.transaction(txn => {
      txn.executeSql(
        'SELECT * FROM tasks',
        [],
```

```
      (tx, results) => {
        const rows = results.rows.raw();
        setTasks(rows);
      },
      error  =>  console.log('Error  fetching
tasks', error)
     );
   });
 };


 const deleteTask = (id) => {
   db.transaction(txn => {
     txn.executeSql(
       'DELETE FROM tasks WHERE id = ?',
       [id],
       () => {
         console.log('Task deleted');
         fetchTasks(); // Reload tasks after
deletion
       },
       error  =>  console.log('Error  deleting
task', error)
     );
   });
 };


 return (
   <View style={styles.container}>
```

```
      <Button title="Add Task" onPress={addTask}
/>

      {tasks.map(task => (
        <View                     key={task.id}
style={styles.taskContainer}>
          <Text>{task.task}</Text>
          <Button  title="Delete"  onPress={()  =>
deleteTask(task.id)} />
        </View>
      ))}
    </View>
  );
};


const styles = StyleSheet.create({
  container: {
    flex: 1,
    justifyContent: 'center',
    alignItems: 'center',
    padding: 20,
  },
  taskContainer: {
    flexDirection: 'row',
    justifyContent: 'space-between',
    margin: 10,
  },
});

export default SQLiteExample;
```

- **Explanation**:
  - The app creates a `tasks` table in the SQLite database if it doesn't already exist.
  - The `addTask` function inserts a new task into the table.
  - The `fetchTasks` function retrieves all tasks and updates the component's state.
  - The `deleteTask` function removes a task by its `id`.

Real-World Example: Creating a To-Do App with Local Data Storage

In this section, we'll combine **AsyncStorage** and **SQLite** to build a simple to-do app. We'll use SQLite for storing tasks persistently in a local database and AsyncStorage to manage the state of the app.

Building the To-Do App

This app will allow users to add, view, and delete tasks, and it will persist the tasks even when the app is closed and reopened.

Example: ToDoApp.js

javascript

```
import React, { useState, useEffect } from
'react';
import { View, Text, TextInput, Button,
StyleSheet, FlatList } from 'react-native';
import SQLite from 'react-native-sqlite-
storage';

const db = SQLite.openDatabase({ name: 'todo.db',
location: 'default' });

const ToDoApp = () => {
  const [task, setTask] = useState('');
  const [tasks, setTasks] = useState([]);

  useEffect(() => {
    db.transaction(txn => {
      txn.executeSql(
        'CREATE TABLE IF NOT EXISTS tasks (id
INTEGER PRIMARY KEY AUTOINCREMENT, task TEXT)',
        [],
        () => console.log('Table created
successfully'),
        error => console.log('Error creating
table', error)
      );
    });
    fetchTasks(); // Load tasks when the app
starts
  }, []);
```

```
const addTask = () => {
  if (task.trim()) {
    db.transaction(txn => {
      txn.executeSql(
        'INSERT INTO tasks (task) VALUES (?)',
        [task],
        () => {
          console.log('Task added');
          setTask('');
          fetchTasks(); // Reload tasks after
adding
        },
        error => console.log('Error adding
task', error)
      );
    });
  }
};

const fetchTasks = () => {
  db.transaction(txn => {
    txn.executeSql(
      'SELECT * FROM tasks',
      [],
      (tx, results) => {
        const rows = results.rows.raw();
        setTasks(rows);
      },
```

```
        error   =>   console.log('Error   fetching
tasks', error)
      );
    });
  };


  const deleteTask = (id) => {
    db.transaction(txn => {
      txn.executeSql(
        'DELETE FROM tasks WHERE id = ?',
        [id],
        () => {
          console.log('Task deleted');
          fetchTasks();  //  Reload  tasks  after
deletion
        },
        error   =>   console.log('Error   deleting
task', error)
      );
    });
  };


  return (
    <View style={styles.container}>
      <TextInput
        style={styles.input}
        placeholder="Add a task"
        value={task}
        onChangeText={setTask}
```

```
      />
      <Button title="Add Task" onPress={addTask}
/>
      <FlatList
        data={tasks}
        keyExtractor={item                    =>
item.id.toString()}
        renderItem={({ item }) => (
          <View style={styles.taskContainer}>
            <Text>{item.task}</Text>
            <Button  title="Delete"  onPress={()
=> deleteTask(item.id)} />
          </View>
        )}
      />
    </View>
  );
};

const styles = StyleSheet.create({
  container: {
    flex: 1,
    justifyContent: 'center',
    alignItems: 'center',
    padding: 20,
  },
  input: {
    height: 40,
    borderColor: 'gray',
```

```
      borderWidth: 1,
      width: '100%',
      marginBottom: 20,
      paddingLeft: 10,
    },
    taskContainer: {
      flexDirection: 'row',
      justifyContent: 'space-between',
      margin: 10,
    },
});


export default ToDoApp;
```

- **Explanation**:
  - The app uses SQLite for persistent storage of tasks.
  - Users can add tasks with a text input, which are then stored in the database.
  - Tasks are displayed in a `FlatList`, which efficiently renders the list of tasks.
  - Each task has a "Delete" button that removes it from the database and updates the UI.

Conclusion

In this chapter, we explored how to persist data locally in React Native using **AsyncStorage** and **SQLite**. **AsyncStorage** is great for simple key-value pairs, while **SQLite** provides a more powerful relational database for complex data. We built a **to-do app** as a real-world example, where users can add, view, and delete tasks, with data being stored persistently across app sessions.

Data persistence is a crucial aspect of mobile app development, and understanding how to store and retrieve data effectively will enable you to create more sophisticated apps. In the next chapters, we will delve deeper into state management, more advanced navigation techniques, and handling user authentication.

CHAPTER 11

HANDLING DEVICE FEATURES IN REACT NATIVE

Mobile apps often need to access native device features such as the **camera**, **GPS**, **notifications**, and other hardware functionalities. React Native provides the ability to interact with these device features, giving you the power to build more interactive and feature-rich apps.

In this chapter, we'll cover how to:

- Access device features like the **camera**, **GPS**, and **notifications**.
- Use **React Native libraries** to interact with native device features.
- Build a **photo gallery app** that allows users to capture photos using the camera.

Accessing Device Features Like Camera, GPS, and Notifications

1. Accessing the Camera

React Native provides access to the camera through various libraries. One of the most popular libraries for working with the

147

camera is **react-native-camera**, but for simplicity and wide usage, we will use **react-native-image-picker**, which allows us to pick images from the gallery or capture new ones using the camera.

Installing react-native-image-picker:

```bash
npm install react-native-image-picker
```

After installing the library, make sure to follow the platform-specific instructions to link the package for iOS and Android.

Example: Using the Camera with react-native-image-picker

```javascript
import React from 'react';
import { View, Button, Image, StyleSheet } from 'react-native';
import { launchCamera } from 'react-native-image-picker';

const CameraExample = () => {
  const [image, setImage] = React.useState(null);
```

```
const takePhoto = () => {
  launchCamera(
    {
      mediaType: 'photo',
      cameraType: 'back',
      quality: 0.5,
    },
    response => {
      if (response.didCancel) {
        console.log('User  cancelled  camera
picker');
      } else if (response.errorCode) {
        console.log('Camera      Error:      ',
response.errorMessage);
      } else {
        const    source    =    {    uri:
response.assets[0].uri };
        setImage(source);
      }
    }
  );
};

return (
  <View style={styles.container}>
    <Button     title="Take     a     Photo"
onPress={takePhoto} />
    {image    &&    <Image    source={image}
style={styles.image} />}
```

```
    </View>
  );
};


const styles = StyleSheet.create({
  container: {
    flex: 1,
    justifyContent: 'center',
    alignItems: 'center',
  },
  image: {
    marginTop: 20,
    width: 200,
    height: 200,
    borderRadius: 10,
  },
});


export default CameraExample;
```

- **Explanation**:
  - launchCamera is used to open the camera and allow the user to take a photo.
  - The response.assets[0].uri contains the URI of the captured photo, which we then use to display the image in an Image component.

150

2. Accessing GPS Location

To get the device's **GPS location**, React Native provides a popular library called **@react-native-community/geolocation**. You can use it to fetch the current location (latitude and longitude) of the device.

Installing the @react-native-community/geolocation library:

```bash
npm install @react-native-community/geolocation
```

Example: Getting the GPS Location

```javascript
import React, { useState } from 'react';
import { View, Text, Button, StyleSheet } from 'react-native';
import Geolocation from '@react-native-community/geolocation';

const LocationExample = () => {
  const [location, setLocation] = useState(null);

  const getLocation = () => {
```

```
  Geolocation.getCurrentPosition(
    position => {
      setLocation(position.coords);
    },
    error => {
      console.log(error);
      alert('Error getting location');
    }
  );
};


return (
  <View style={styles.container}>
    <Button    title="Get    Current    Location"
onPress={getLocation} />
    {location && (
      <Text>
        Latitude:         {location.latitude},
Longitude: {location.longitude}
      </Text>
    )}
  </View>
);
};


const styles = StyleSheet.create({
  container: {
    flex: 1,
    justifyContent: 'center',
```

```
  alignItems: 'center',
  padding: 20,
 },
});
```

```
export default LocationExample;
```

- **Explanation**:
  - o The `getCurrentPosition` method fetches the device's current location, which we use to display the latitude and longitude.
  - o If the GPS is unavailable or there's an error, we show an alert message.

3. Accessing Push Notifications

Push notifications are an essential feature for many mobile apps, and React Native provides libraries such as **react-native-push-notification** or **react-native-firebase** to handle notifications.

For this chapter, we'll use **react-native-push-notification** to send and handle local push notifications.

Installing `react-native-push-notification`:

```bash
```

```
npm install react-native-push-notification
```

153

Make sure to follow the library's setup instructions for iOS and Android.

Example: Sending a Local Notification

```javascript

import React from 'react';
import { View, Button, StyleSheet } from 'react-native';
import PushNotification from 'react-native-push-notification';

const NotificationExample = () => {
  const sendNotification = () => {
    PushNotification.localNotification({
      title: 'Sample Notification',
      message: 'This is a test notification.',
    });
  };

  return (
    <View style={styles.container}>
      <Button       title="Send      Notification"
onPress={sendNotification} />
    </View>
  );
};
```

```
const styles = StyleSheet.create({
  container: {
    flex: 1,
    justifyContent: 'center',
    alignItems: 'center',
  },
});
```

```
export default NotificationExample;
```

- **Explanation**:
    - o The `localNotification` method sends a local notification to the device.
    - o The notification includes a title and message, which will be shown in the device's notification center.

Real-World Example: Building a Photo Gallery App with Camera Access

Let's now combine the knowledge we've gained so far and build a **Photo Gallery App** where users can take pictures and view them in a gallery-style layout.

Creating the Photo Gallery App

This app will:

- Allow users to take photos using the camera.

- Display the captured photos in a gallery layout.

Example: PhotoGalleryApp.js

```javascript
import React, { useState } from 'react';
import { View, Text, Button, Image, FlatList,
StyleSheet } from 'react-native';
import { launchCamera } from 'react-native-image-
picker';

const PhotoGalleryApp = () => {
  const [photos, setPhotos] = useState([]);

  const takePhoto = () => {
    launchCamera(
      {
        mediaType: 'photo',
        cameraType: 'back',
        quality: 0.5,
      },
      response => {
        if (response.didCancel) {
          console.log('User    cancelled    camera
picker');
        } else if (response.errorCode) {
```

156

```
        console.log('Camera      Error:      ',
response.errorMessage);
      } else {
        const    newPhoto    =    {    uri:
response.assets[0].uri };
        setPhotos(prevPhotos           =>
[...prevPhotos, newPhoto]);
      }
    }
   );
 };


 const renderItem = ({ item }) => (
   <View style={styles.photoContainer}>
     <Image  source={item}  style={styles.photo}
/>
   </View>
 );


 return (
   <View style={styles.container}>
     <Text          style={styles.title}>Photo
Gallery</Text>
     <Button    title="Take    a    Photo"
onPress={takePhoto} />
     <FlatList
       data={photos}
       renderItem={renderItem}
```

157

```
      keyExtractor={(item,       index)       =>
index.toString()}
        numColumns={3}
      />
    </View>
  );
};


const styles = StyleSheet.create({
  container: {
    flex: 1,
    justifyContent: 'center',
    alignItems: 'center',
    padding: 20,
  },
  title: {
    fontSize: 24,
    fontWeight: 'bold',
    marginBottom: 20,
  },
  photoContainer: {
    margin: 5,
  },
  photo: {
    width: 100,
    height: 100,
    borderRadius: 8,
  },
});
```

```
export default PhotoGalleryApp;
```

- **Explanation**:

    o **takePhoto**: This function opens the camera and lets the user take a photo. The captured photo is then added to the `photos` array in the state.

    o **FlatList**: We use `FlatList` to display the images in a gallery-style layout, with three photos per row.

    o **Styling**: The images are displayed with a margin, and each image is given a width and height of 100, along with rounded corners using `borderRadius`.

Conclusion

In this chapter, we covered how to access device features in React Native, including the **camera**, **GPS**, and **push notifications**. We also explored how to interact with these features using libraries like `react-native-image-picker`, `@react-native-community/geolocation`, and `react-native-push-notification`.

We then applied this knowledge by building a **photo gallery app** that allows users to capture photos and view them in a gallery. By leveraging device features, you can create rich, interactive mobile applications that provide a seamless user experience.

In the following chapters, we'll continue to explore more advanced features like handling complex forms, working with third-party libraries, and integrating external APIs.

CHAPTER 12

DEBUGGING AND ERROR HANDLING IN REACT NATIVE

Debugging and error handling are crucial skills in app development, especially when building mobile apps where issues can be harder to detect due to the nature of the platform. React Native offers several tools and techniques for debugging issues and handling errors effectively. In this chapter, we will cover:

- Using **Chrome DevTools** and **React Native Debugger** for debugging.
- Handling errors in React Native with **try/catch** blocks and **Error Boundaries**.
- A real-world example of debugging an issue in a list rendering app.

Using Chrome DevTools and React Native Debugger

1. Chrome DevTools

Chrome DevTools is a powerful suite of debugging tools that allow you to inspect and debug JavaScript code in React Native. You can use DevTools to:

161

- View logs.
- Set breakpoints.
- Profile your app's performance.
- Inspect the components.

Enabling Chrome DevTools in React Native

To use Chrome DevTools for debugging, you need to run the app in debug mode. Follow these steps:

1. **Start the app** in development mode by running:

```bash

npx react-native run-android     // for Android
npx react-native run-ios       // for iOS
```

2. Once the app is running, **shake the device** (or press **Cmd + D** on iOS or **Cmd + M** on Android) to open the **React Native DevMenu**.
3. In the menu, select **"Debug"**. This will open Chrome with the developer tools.

In the browser, open the **Console** tab in DevTools to view the logs. This will show any `console.log` output from your app, and you can also use `debugger;` to set breakpoints.

Using `console.log` for Debugging:

162

```
javascript

console.log('Current state:', this.state);
```

This simple method helps you track the state and behavior of your app during development.

2. React Native Debugger

React Native Debugger is a standalone debugger for React Native that integrates well with the **Redux DevTools**, offering an enhanced debugging experience. It combines the power of Chrome DevTools with React-specific features and more.

Installing React Native Debugger

1. Download **React Native Debugger** from the official repository: https://github.com/jhen0409/react-native-debugger.
2. Once installed, open the React Native Debugger and then run your app.

Connecting React Native Debugger:

1. Open the **DevMenu** in the app (shake the device or press Cmd + D for iOS, Cmd + M for Android).
2. Enable **Remote Debugging**. The app will now connect to React Native Debugger.

163

React Native Debugger provides tools like:

- **Network inspector** for monitoring API calls.
- **Console logging** with color-coded logs for easier debugging.
- **Redux state inspection** for apps using Redux.

Handling Errors in React Native

1. Using `try/catch` for Error Handling

The `try/catch` statement is commonly used to handle errors in JavaScript. It allows you to attempt to execute a block of code and catch any errors that might occur during the execution.

Basic Syntax of `try/catch`:

```javascript
try {
  // Code that might throw an error
} catch (error) {
  // Handle the error
  console.error(error);
}
```

Example: Using `try/catch` in React Native

```javascript
```

```
import React, { useState } from 'react';
import { View, Button, Text, StyleSheet } from
'react-native';

const TryCatchExample = () => {
  const [message, setMessage] = useState('');

  const handleError = () => {
    try {
      // Simulate a function that throws an error
      throw new Error('Something went wrong!');
    } catch (error) {
      setMessage(error.message);  // Set error
message in state
      console.log(error);
    }
  };

  return (
    <View style={styles.container}>
      <Button title="Trigger Error"
onPress={handleError} />
      {message && <Text
style={styles.errorText}>{message}</Text>}
    </View>
  );
};
```

165

```
const styles = StyleSheet.create({
  container: {
    flex: 1,
    justifyContent: 'center',
    alignItems: 'center',
  },
  errorText: {
    marginTop: 20,
    color: 'red',
  },
});
```

```
export default TryCatchExample;
```

- **Explanation**:
  - o   `try` attempts to execute the code inside the block.
  - o   If an error occurs (like the `throw new Error()`), the `catch` block catches it and handles it (in this case, by setting the error message in the state and logging it).

2. Using Error Boundaries

In React, **Error Boundaries** are special components that catch errors in their child components, preventing the entire app from crashing. Error boundaries are a React concept that you can use in React Native as well.

An **Error Boundary** can catch JavaScript errors in its child components, log those errors, and display a fallback UI.

Example: Creating an Error Boundary

```javascript
import React, { Component } from 'react';
import { View, Text, Button, StyleSheet } from
'react-native';

class ErrorBoundary extends Component {
  state = { hasError: false, errorMessage: '' };

  static getDerivedStateFromError(error) {
    return { hasError: true, errorMessage:
error.message };
  }

  componentDidCatch(error, info) {
    console.log(error, info);
  }

  render() {
    if (this.state.hasError) {
      return                              <Text
style={styles.errorText}>Something went wrong:
{this.state.errorMessage}</Text>;
    }
```

```
      return this.props.children;
  }
}

const FaultyComponent = () => {
  throw new Error('This is a simulated error');
};

const App = () => {
  return (
    <ErrorBoundary>
      <View style={styles.container}>
        <Text>No errors yet!</Text>
        <FaultyComponent />
      </View>
    </ErrorBoundary>
  );
};

const styles = StyleSheet.create({
  container: {
    flex: 1,
    justifyContent: 'center',
    alignItems: 'center',
  },
  errorText: {
    color: 'red',
    fontSize: 16,
  },
```

```
});
```

```
export default App;
```

- **Explanation**:
    - o The `ErrorBoundary` component catches any errors that occur in its child components.
    - o If an error is thrown (as simulated in `FaultyComponent`), the `ErrorBoundary` component catches the error, logs it, and renders a fallback UI (`Something went wrong` message).

Real-World Example: Debugging an Issue in a List Rendering App

In this real-world example, we will build a simple **list rendering app** where we dynamically render a list of items. We will then introduce an error to simulate a problem and debug it using the tools and techniques discussed.

Example: List Rendering App with Debugging

```javascript
import React, { useState, useEffect } from
'react';
```

```
import { View, Text, FlatList, Button, StyleSheet
} from 'react-native';

const ListRenderingApp = () => {
  const [items, setItems] = useState([]);
  const [error, setError] = useState(null);

  useEffect(() => {
    try {
      // Simulating a network request that
fetches data
      const fetchedItems = ['Item 1', 'Item 2',
'Item 3'];
      if (!fetchedItems) {
        throw new Error('Failed to fetch items');
      }
      setItems(fetchedItems);
    } catch (err) {
      setError(err.message);
    }
  }, []);

  const handleRemoveItem = index => {
    const newItems = items.filter((item, idx) =>
idx !== index);
    setItems(newItems);
  };

  if (error) {
```

170

```
    return                         <Text
style={styles.errorText}>{error}</Text>;
  }

  return (
    <View style={styles.container}>
      <Text      style={styles.title}>List      of
Items</Text>
      <FlatList
        data={items}
        keyExtractor={(item,       index)       =>
index.toString()}
        renderItem={({ item, index }) => (
          <View style={styles.itemContainer}>
            <Text>{item}</Text>
            <Button  title="Remove"  onPress={()
=> handleRemoveItem(index)} />
          </View>
        )}
      />
    </View>
  );
};

const styles = StyleSheet.create({
  container: {
    flex: 1,
    padding: 20,
  },
```

```
title: {
  fontSize: 20,
  fontWeight: 'bold',
  marginBottom: 10,
},
itemContainer: {
  flexDirection: 'row',
  justifyContent: 'space-between',
  marginBottom: 10,
},
errorText: {
  color: 'red',
  fontSize: 18,
},
});

export default ListRenderingApp;
```

Debugging the Issue:

- The app initially fetches a list of items and displays them in a FlatList.
- If the fetch fails, an error is thrown and caught by the catch block.
- We simulate an error by checking if the fetched data exists, and if not, we throw an error.
- The error message is displayed in the UI.

Conclusion

In this chapter, we learned how to debug React Native apps using **Chrome DevTools** and **React Native Debugger**. We explored error handling techniques such as using `try/catch` blocks and implementing **Error Boundaries** for graceful error recovery in React Native apps.

We also built a **real-world list rendering app** and debugged a simulated issue using the techniques we've covered. Debugging and error handling are essential for building reliable mobile applications, and mastering these techniques will help you resolve issues quickly and maintain a smooth user experience.

In the following chapters, we'll continue to explore advanced topics in React Native, including working with third-party libraries, optimizing performance, and improving app reliability.

Part 4

Advanced Concepts in React Native

CHAPTER 13

PERFORMANCE OPTIMIZATION IN REACT NATIVE

In this chapter, we will explore how to optimize the performance of your React Native applications. Optimizing performance is crucial, especially as your app grows in size and complexity. Mobile apps, particularly those that deal with large data sets, need to be efficient in rendering components, managing memory, and ensuring a smooth user experience.

We will focus on:

- **Optimizing rendering performance** using `shouldComponentUpdate` and `React.memo`.
- **Using `FlatList`** for rendering large data sets efficiently and reducing unnecessary re-renders.
- A **real-world example** of optimizing a scrollable list of items.

Optimizing Rendering Performance with shouldComponentUpdate *and* React.memo

1. shouldComponentUpdate in Class Components

In **class components**, React provides the **shouldComponentUpdate** lifecycle method to control whether a component should re-render based on changes in props or state. This method allows you to return false when you don't want the component to re-render, thus optimizing performance by preventing unnecessary renders.

Basic Usage of shouldComponentUpdate:

javascript

```javascript
class MyComponent extends React.Component {
  shouldComponentUpdate(nextProps, nextState) {
    if (nextProps.value === this.props.value) {
      return false; // Prevent re-render if value
hasn't changed
    }
    return true;
  }

  render() {
    return <Text>{this.props.value}</Text>;
  }
}
```

- **Explanation**:
  - The `shouldComponentUpdate` method compares the new and current props. If they are the same, the method returns `false`, preventing the component from re-rendering. If the props have changed, it returns `true`, allowing the component to re-render.

2. React.memo for Functional Components

In **functional components**, you can achieve similar performance optimization with **React.memo**. React.memo is a higher-order component that memorizes the component's output and only re-renders the component when its props change.

Basic Usage of React.memo:

javascript

```javascript
const MyComponent = React.memo(({ value }) => {
  console.log('Rendering:', value);
  return <Text>{value}</Text>;
});
```

- **Explanation**:
  - React.memo wraps the MyComponent function and prevents it from re-rendering unless the value prop changes.

177

o   If the component's props remain the same, React skips the render, improving performance.

Custom Comparison with `React.memo`: You can also provide a custom comparison function to fine-tune when a component should re-render.

javascript

```
const MyComponent = React.memo(({ value }) => {
  console.log('Rendering:', value);
  return <Text>{value}</Text>;
}, (prevProps, nextProps) => {
  return prevProps.value === nextProps.value;  //
Custom comparison
});
```

- **Explanation**:
    o   The second argument to `React.memo` is a function that compares the current and next props. If the function returns `true`, React skips the re-render.

Using `FlatList` for Large Data Sets and Reducing Re-renders

When dealing with large lists of data, rendering every item at once can severely degrade performance. React Native provides

FlatList, which is optimized for rendering large data sets efficiently by only rendering the visible items and reusing the items that go off-screen.

Key Features of FlatList:

1. **initialNumToRender**: Controls how many items to render initially.

2. **maxToRenderPerBatch**: Limits the number of items rendered in one batch.

3. **windowSize**: Defines how many items should be kept in memory before and after the visible area.

4. **getItemLayout**: Helps React Native calculate item positions for efficient scrolling (especially for fixed-height items).

5. **keyExtractor**: Allows you to define the key for each item to optimize updates and re-renders.

Basic Usage of FlatList:

```javascript
import React from 'react';
import { View, Text, FlatList, StyleSheet } from
'react-native';

const data = Array.from({ length: 1000 }, (_,
index) => ({
```

```
  id: index.toString(),
  title: `Item ${index + 1}`,
}));

const ListExample = () => {
  return (
    <FlatList
      data={data}
      renderItem={({ item }) => (
        <View style={styles.item}>
          <Text>{item.title}</Text>
        </View>
      )}
      keyExtractor={(item) => item.id}
      initialNumToRender={10} // Render 10 items
initially
      maxToRenderPerBatch={10}   //   Render   10
items per batch
      windowSize={5} // Render 5 items before and
after the viewport
    />
  );
};

const styles = StyleSheet.create({
  item: {
    padding: 20,
    borderBottomWidth: 1,
    borderBottomColor: '#ccc',
```

```
    },
});
```

```
export default ListExample;
```

- **Explanation**:
    - o   `FlatList` is used to render a list of 1,000 items, but it only renders the visible items plus a few extra for smoother scrolling.
    - o   **keyExtractor** ensures each item has a unique identifier, which helps optimize rendering.
    - o   **initialNumToRender** limits the number of items rendered initially for faster loading.

Optimizing `FlatList` with `getItemLayout`

If you have a list with fixed-height items, you can use the `getItemLayout` prop to optimize the rendering and scrolling performance further. This allows React Native to calculate the position of each item without rendering the entire list.

Example: Using getItemLayout with FlatList

```javascript
import React from 'react';
import { View, Text, FlatList, StyleSheet } from
'react-native';
```

```
const data = Array.from({ length: 1000 }, (_,
index) => ({
  id: index.toString(),
  title: `Item ${index + 1}`,
}));

const ListExample = () => {
  return (
    <FlatList
      data={data}
      renderItem={({ item }) => (
        <View style={styles.item}>
          <Text>{item.title}</Text>
        </View>
      )}
      keyExtractor={(item) => item.id}
      getItemLayout={(data, index) => ({
        length: 50, // Height of each item
        offset: 50 * index, // Position of the
item
        index,
      })}
    />
  );
};

const styles = StyleSheet.create({
  item: {
```

```
  padding: 20,
  height: 50, // Fixed height for each item
  borderBottomWidth: 1,
  borderBottomColor: '#ccc',
 },
});
```

```
export default ListExample;
```

- **Explanation**:
  o The getItemLayout function is used to specify the height (length) and position (offset) of each item in the list. This allows React Native to efficiently calculate the positions of items during scrolling without rendering the entire list.

Real-World Example: Optimizing a Scrollable List of Items

In this real-world example, we'll build a simple **to-do list app** using FlatList. We will apply performance optimizations to ensure smooth scrolling even with a large number of tasks.

Optimizing the To-Do List App

Example: OptimizedToDoApp.js

```
javascript
```

```
import React, { useState, useCallback } from
'react';
import { View, Text, FlatList, Button, StyleSheet
} from 'react-native';

const OptimizedToDoApp = () => {
  const [tasks, setTasks] = useState(
    Array.from({ length: 1000 }, (_, index) => ({
      id: index.toString(),
      title: `Task ${index + 1}`,
    }))
  );

  const handleAddTask = () => {
    setTasks((prevTasks) => [
      ...prevTasks,
      { id: (prevTasks.length + 1).toString(),
title: `New Task ${prevTasks.length + 1}` },
    ]);
  };

  const renderItem = useCallback(
    ({ item }) => (
      <View style={styles.item}>
        <Text>{item.title}</Text>
      </View>
    ),
    []
  );
```

184

```
  return (
    <View style={styles.container}>
      <Button         title="Add          Task"
onPress={handleAddTask} />
      <FlatList
        data={tasks}
        renderItem={renderItem}
        keyExtractor={(item) => item.id}
        initialNumToRender={10}
        maxToRenderPerBatch={10}
        windowSize={5}
        getItemLayout={(data, index) => ({
          length: 50,
          offset: 50 * index,
          index,
        })}
      />
    </View>
  );
};

const styles = StyleSheet.create({
  container: {
    flex: 1,
    justifyContent: 'center',
    padding: 20,
  },
  item: {
```

```
    padding: 20,
    height: 50,
    borderBottomWidth: 1,
    borderBottomColor: '#ccc',
  },
});
```

```
export default OptimizedToDoApp;
```

- **Explanation**:
  - o **FlatList** is used to render a large list of tasks (1,000 items).
  - o **initialNumToRender** and **maxToRenderPerBatch** help control how many items are rendered at once.
  - o **windowSize** specifies how many items should be kept in memory before and after the visible area.
  - o **getItemLayout** optimizes performance by providing fixed layout information, preventing React Native from needing to calculate the positions dynamically.

Conclusion

In this chapter, we learned how to optimize the performance of React Native apps, particularly when rendering large data sets. We explored:

- `shouldComponentUpdate` and `React.memo` for preventing unnecessary re-renders in class and functional components.
- `FlatList` for efficiently rendering large lists by limiting the number of items rendered and optimizing memory usage.
- A real-world example of **optimizing a scrollable list** with performance tweaks.

Performance optimization is essential for building smooth, responsive mobile apps, especially when dealing with large data sets. In the next chapters, we'll continue exploring advanced concepts like working with complex forms, third-party libraries, and advanced navigation techniques.

CHAPTER 14

ANIMATIONS IN REACT NATIVE

Animations can significantly enhance the user experience of your app, making it feel more interactive, engaging, and responsive. React Native provides a powerful suite of tools to add animations to your app, allowing you to create smooth transitions and visual effects.

In this chapter, we will cover:

- An **introduction to React Native animations**.
- How to use the **Animated API** for smooth transitions and animations.
- A **real-world example** where we add animations to a button click interaction to demonstrate how animations can be incorporated into your app.

Introduction to React Native Animations

React Native offers two main animation libraries for building animations:

188

1. **Animated API**: A low-level API that provides fine control over animations, ideal for building custom animations or controlling complex transitions.

2. **LayoutAnimation**: A simpler, higher-level API for animating changes to layout, such as resizing or repositioning components.

For this chapter, we'll focus on the **Animated API**, which offers more flexibility and control.

How the Animated API Works

The `Animated` API provides a set of tools to animate values (e.g., position, opacity, scale) over time. You can animate any numeric value (such as width, height, opacity) and bind them to styles that are applied to the component.

Here are some key components of the `Animated` API:

- **`Animated.View`**: A wrapper around the standard `View` component that supports animations.
- **`Animated.Value`**: A mutable value that can be animated over time.
- **`Animated.timing`**: A method for animating values over a set duration.
- **`Animated.spring`**: A method for spring-based animations that mimic real-world physics.

189

- **Animated.sequence**: A method for running multiple animations in sequence.

- **Animated.parallel**: A method for running animations simultaneously.

Using the Animated API for Smooth Transitions

1. Creating an Animated Value

First, create an **Animated.Value** to represent a dynamic property, such as opacity or position.

```javascript
const animation = new Animated.Value(0);   // Initial value is 0
```

You can bind this value to a style property, such as opacity, to control the opacity of a component.

2. Animating with Animated.timing

To create a smooth transition, use the **Animated.timing** method. This method animates a value over a specific duration.

```javascript
Animated.timing(animation, {
```

190

```
    toValue: 1,              // Target value
    duration: 500,               // Duration of the
animation (in milliseconds)
    useNativeDriver: true // Enable native driver
for performance
}).start();
```

In the above code, the opacity will animate from 0 to 1 over 500 milliseconds.

3. Binding to Styles

Once the animated value is set up, bind it to the component's style. For example, you can animate the opacity or translateX (position) of a View component.

```javascript

<Animated.View
  style={{
    opacity: animation, // Binding the animated
value to opacity
  }}
>
  <Text>Animated Text</Text>
</Animated.View>
```

4. Combining Animations

You can combine multiple animations to create more complex transitions. For instance, animating both opacity and position at the same time.

```javascript
Animated.parallel([
  Animated.timing(animation, { toValue: 1,
duration: 500 }),
  Animated.timing(position, { toValue: 200,
duration: 500 }),
]).start();
```

- **Explanation**:
  - o In this example, both the opacity and the position of a component will animate simultaneously.

Real-World Example: Adding Animations to a Button Click Interaction

Now, let's create a simple button that animates a View when clicked. We'll animate the button's scale and opacity when it's pressed, and we'll use **Animated.timing** to smoothly transition these values.

Creating a Button Animation

Example: Animated Button Click Interaction

```javascript

import React, { useState } from 'react';
import { View, Text, TouchableOpacity, Animated,
StyleSheet } from 'react-native';

const ButtonAnimationExample = () => {
  const      [animation]      =      useState(new
Animated.Value(1)); // Initial scale value

  // Function to trigger the animation on button
press
  const handlePress = () => {
    // Animate the scale and opacity when the
button is pressed
    Animated.sequence([
      Animated.timing(animation, {
        toValue: 0.8,  // Scale down to 80%
        duration: 200, // Duration of animation
        useNativeDriver: true,
      }),
      Animated.timing(animation, {
        toValue: 1,    // Scale back to 100%
        duration: 200, // Duration of animation
        useNativeDriver: true,
      }),
```

```
      ]).start();
  };


  return (
    <View style={styles.container}>
      <TouchableOpacity onPress={handlePress}>
        <Animated.View
          style={[
            styles.button,
            {
              transform: [{ scale: animation }],
// Apply animated scale
            },
          ]}
        >
          <Text  style={styles.buttonText}>Press
Me</Text>
        </Animated.View>
      </TouchableOpacity>
    </View>
  );
};


const styles = StyleSheet.create({
  container: {
    flex: 1,
    justifyContent: 'center',
    alignItems: 'center',
  },
```

```
button: {
  backgroundColor: '#3498db',
  padding: 20,
  borderRadius: 10,
},
buttonText: {
  color: 'white',
  fontSize: 18,
},
});
```

```
export default ButtonAnimationExample;
```

- **Explanation**:
  - The `animation` state is initialized with a value of 1 (no scaling).
  - When the user presses the button, the `handlePress` function triggers the animation.
  - **Animated.sequence** is used to animate the button first scaling down to 0.8 (80% of its original size), then scaling back up to 1.
  - **transform: [{ scale: animation }]** binds the animated value to the scale transformation of the `Animated.View` component.

195

How It Works:

- When the user presses the button, it will shrink slightly (scale to 80%) and then return to its original size (scale to 100%).
- This gives the user a visual cue that the button has been pressed, enhancing the interaction.

Enhancing the Animation: Adding Opacity

To make the animation even more interactive, let's also animate the **opacity** of the button so that it fades slightly when pressed.

Updated Example with Opacity:

javascript

```
import React, { useState } from 'react';
import { View, Text, TouchableOpacity, Animated,
StyleSheet } from 'react-native';

const ButtonAnimationExample = () => {
  const      [animation]      =      useState(new
Animated.Value(1)); // Initial scale value

  // Function to trigger the animation on button
press
  const handlePress = () => {
```

```
    // Animate the scale and opacity when the
button is pressed
    Animated.sequence([
      Animated.timing(animation, {
        toValue: 0.8,   // Scale down to 80%
        duration: 200, // Duration of animation
        useNativeDriver: true,
      }),
      Animated.timing(animation, {
        toValue: 1,     // Scale back to 100%
        duration: 200, // Duration of animation
        useNativeDriver: true,
      }),
    ]).start();
  };


  return (
    <View style={styles.container}>
      <TouchableOpacity onPress={handlePress}>
        <Animated.View
          style={[
            styles.button,
            {
              transform: [{ scale: animation }],
// Apply animated scale
              opacity: animation,  //  Apply
animated opacity
            },
          ]}
```

```
        >
          <Text  style={styles.buttonText}>Press
Me</Text>
        </Animated.View>
      </TouchableOpacity>
    </View>
  );
};

const styles = StyleSheet.create({
  container: {
    flex: 1,
    justifyContent: 'center',
    alignItems: 'center',
  },
  button: {
    backgroundColor: '#3498db',
    padding: 20,
    borderRadius: 10,
  },
  buttonText: {
    color: 'white',
    fontSize: 18,
  },
});

export default ButtonAnimationExample;
```

- **Explanation**:

o The opacity is also animated along with the scale. Now, when the user presses the button, it will slightly shrink and fade out before returning to its original size and opacity.

o The **opacity** changes in sync with the **scale**, making the button press feel even more interactive.

Conclusion

In this chapter, we explored how to use the **Animated API** in React Native to add smooth animations to your app. We covered:

- **Basic animation** techniques using `Animated.timing` for transitions like scale and opacity.
- How to use **`React.memo`** and **`shouldComponentUpdate`** to optimize rendering performance when working with animated components.
- A **real-world example** of adding animations to a button click interaction to make the user experience more interactive.

Animations are a powerful way to improve user interaction in your app, making it feel smoother and more intuitive. In the next chapters, we'll explore more advanced animation techniques, performance optimization, and how to integrate animations into complex workflows.

CHAPTER 15

CUSTOM COMPONENTS AND NATIVE MODULES

In this chapter, we'll cover how to extend React Native's capabilities by building **custom components** and integrating **native code** using **Native Modules**. React Native is a powerful framework for building mobile applications, but sometimes you need to create custom UI components or interact with native device functionality that isn't available in the default library. This chapter will guide you through creating custom components and using **Native Modules** to access native device functionality.

By the end of this chapter, you will have a strong understanding of:

- **Building custom components** in React Native to meet specific needs.
- **Integrating native code** with React Native using **Native Modules** to access device-specific features that are not provided out of the box.
- A **real-world example** of building a custom button component and integrating native code to enhance its functionality.

Building Custom Components in React Native

React Native allows you to create custom components just like in React. Custom components help to organize and encapsulate specific pieces of functionality in your app, making the code more reusable and easier to maintain.

1. Creating a Custom Component

A custom component in React Native is simply a JavaScript function or class that returns a React Native component (such as View, Text, or Image) or a combination of these.

Example: Basic Custom Button Component

```javascript
import React from 'react';
import { View, Text, TouchableOpacity, StyleSheet
} from 'react-native';

const CustomButton = ({ onPress, title, color })
=> {
  return (
    <TouchableOpacity          onPress={onPress}
style={{[styles.button, { backgroundColor: color
}]}>
      <Text
style={styles.buttonText}>{title}</Text>
```

```
    </TouchableOpacity>
  );
};


const styles = StyleSheet.create({
  button: {
    padding: 10,
    borderRadius: 5,
    alignItems: 'center',
  },
  buttonText: {
    color: 'white',
    fontSize: 16,
  },
});


export default CustomButton;
```

- **Explanation**:
  o The CustomButton component is a functional component that takes onPress, title, and color as props.
  o TouchableOpacity is used to create a touchable button, and Text is used to display the button's label.
  o The button's style is dynamically set using the color prop, which allows different buttons to have different background colors.

2. Using the Custom Component

You can now use this custom button in other parts of your app.

Example: Using Custom Button in an App

javascript

```
import React from 'react';
import { View, Alert, StyleSheet } from 'react-native';
import CustomButton from './CustomButton'; // Import the CustomButton component

const App = () => {
  const showAlert = () => {
    Alert.alert('Button Clicked!', 'You have clicked the custom button.');
  };

  return (
    <View style={styles.container}>
      <CustomButton title="Click Me" onPress={showAlert} color="blue" />
      <CustomButton title="Another Button" onPress={showAlert} color="green" />
    </View>
  );
};
```

```
const styles = StyleSheet.create({
  container: {
    flex: 1,
    justifyContent: 'center',
    alignItems: 'center',
  },
});
```

```
export default App;
```

- **Explanation**:
  - o Here, we use the `CustomButton` twice, with different colors and titles.
  - o When the button is pressed, the `showAlert` function is called, displaying an alert.

Integrating Native Code with React Native Using Native Modules

In React Native, you may need to access device-specific features that are not available through the JavaScript APIs. To do this, you can integrate **native code** written in **Java** (for Android) or **Objective-C/Swift** (for iOS) into your React Native app using **Native Modules**.

1. What Are Native Modules?

A **Native Module** is a bridge between JavaScript and native code, allowing you to call native methods directly from JavaScript. Native Modules allow React Native to access platform-specific functionality that is not available in the core React Native library.

2. Creating a Native Module

To create a Native Module, you need to:

1. Write a native module in Java (for Android) or Objective-C/Swift (for iOS).
2. Expose the native methods to React Native via a bridge.
3. Call the native methods from your JavaScript code.

Let's go through a simple example of creating a custom button that integrates native code to show a custom toast message on both Android and iOS.

Real-World Example: Building a Custom Button with Native Code Integration

In this example, we'll create a **custom button** that, when pressed, shows a **native toast message**. We will implement the native module for both Android and iOS.

Step 1: Android Native Module (Toast)

For Android, we need to create a native module that shows a toast message when called from JavaScript.

1. Create a new Java class that extends ReactContextBaseJavaModule.
2. Implement the required method to show the toast.

Example: Android Native Module (ToastModule.java)

```java
package com.custombuttonmodule;

import android.widget.Toast;
import com.facebook.react.bridge.ReactApplicationContext;
import com.facebook.react.bridge.ReactContextBaseJavaModule;
import com.facebook.react.bridge.ReactMethod;

public class ToastModule extends ReactContextBaseJavaModule {

    public ToastModule(ReactApplicationContext reactContext) {
```

```
        super(reactContext);
    }

    @Override
    public String getName() {
        return "ToastModule";
    }

    @ReactMethod
    public void showToast(String message) {

Toast.makeText(getReactApplicationContext(),
message, Toast.LENGTH_SHORT).show();
    }
}
```

- **Explanation**:
  - ToastModule defines a showToast method that shows a toast message on Android.
  - The @ReactMethod decorator exposes the showToast method to JavaScript.

3. Register the module in the package.

Example: Package Registration (ToastModulePackage.java)

java

```
package com.custombuttonmodule;
```

```java
import com.facebook.react.ReactPackage;
import
com.facebook.react.bridge.ReactApplicationConte
xt;
import
com.facebook.react.bridge.ReactContextBaseJavaM
odule;
import
com.facebook.react.bridge.ReactModuleProvider;
import com.facebook.react.uimanager.ViewManager;
import com.facebook.react.bridge.NativeModule;
import java.util.Collections;
import java.util.List;

public    class    ToastModulePackage    implements
ReactPackage {
    @Override
    public                      List<NativeModule>
createNativeModules(ReactApplicationContext
reactContext) {
        return    Collections.singletonList(new
ToastModule(reactContext));
    }

    @Override
    public                      List<ViewManager>
createViewManagers(ReactApplicationContext
reactContext) {
```

```
        return Collections.emptyList();
    }
}
```

- **Explanation**:
    - o The `ToastModulePackage` is responsible for registering the `ToastModule` so that it can be accessed from JavaScript.

Step 2: iOS Native Module (Toast)

For iOS, we need to create a similar native module that shows a toast message using **Objective-C** or **Swift**.

Example: iOS Native Module (ToastModule.m)

```objc
objc

#import <React/RCTBridgeModule.h>
#import <UIKit/UIKit.h>

@interface      ToastModule      :      NSObject
<RCTBridgeModule>
@end

@implementation ToastModule

RCT_EXPORT_MODULE();
```

210

```
RCT_EXPORT_METHOD(showToast:(NSString *)message)
{
  UIAlertController *alert = [UIAlertController
alertControllerWithTitle:@"Toast"

message:message

preferredStyle:UIAlertControllerStyleAlert];
  UIViewController *vc = [[[[UIApplication
sharedApplication] delegate] window]
rootViewController];
  [vc presentViewController:alert animated:YES
completion:nil];
  [alert
performSelector:@selector(dismissViewController
Animated:completion:) withObject:nil
afterDelay:2];
}

@end
```

- **Explanation**:
  - showToast uses UIAlertController to show a toast-like message on iOS.
  - RCT_EXPORT_METHOD exposes the method to JavaScript.

Step 3: Using the Native Module in JavaScript

Now that we have set up our native modules for both platforms, we can use them in our React Native JavaScript code.

Example: Using the Custom Button with Native Module Integration

```javascript
import React from 'react';
import { View, Text, TouchableOpacity, StyleSheet
} from 'react-native';
import { NativeModules } from 'react-native';

const { ToastModule } = NativeModules;

const CustomButtonWithNativeModule = () => {
  const handlePress = () => {
    ToastModule.showToast('Hello    from    Native
Toast!');
  };

  return (
    <View style={styles.container}>
      <TouchableOpacity    onPress={handlePress}
style={styles.button}>
        <Text    style={styles.buttonText}>Press
Me</Text>
```

```
      </TouchableOpacity>
    </View>
  );
};


const styles = StyleSheet.create({
  container: {
    flex: 1,
    justifyContent: 'center',
    alignItems: 'center',
  },
  button: {
    backgroundColor: '#3498db',
    padding: 20,
    borderRadius: 10,
  },
  buttonText: {
    color: 'white',
    fontSize: 18,
  },
});


export default CustomButtonWithNativeModule;
```

- **Explanation**:
  - The `ToastModule` is imported from `NativeModules` and used to call the `showToast` method when the button is pressed.

213

o This triggers the native code to show a toast message on Android and iOS.

Conclusion

In this chapter, we explored:

- How to build **custom components** in React Native to encapsulate and reuse functionality.
- How to integrate **native code** using **Native Modules** to access platform-specific features not available in the core React Native library.
- A **real-world example** where we built a custom button and integrated native code for displaying toast messages on both Android and iOS.

Native Modules are a powerful tool for extending React Native's capabilities, and they allow you to integrate deeply with native device functionality. In the next chapters, we will explore more advanced features like handling background tasks, integrating third-party libraries, and optimizing app performance.

214

CHAPTER 16

HANDLING BACKGROUND TASKS AND NOTIFICATIONS

In modern mobile applications, certain tasks need to continue running even when the app is not in the foreground. For example, syncing data, sending notifications, and monitoring location updates are tasks that require background execution. React Native provides libraries and strategies for managing background tasks and handling notifications to enhance the functionality and user experience of your app.

In this chapter, we will explore:

- Managing **background tasks** with **React Native Background Fetch**.
- Sending **local** and **push notifications**.
- A **real-world example** where we implement background data sync with push notifications.

Managing Background Tasks with React Native Background Fetch

Background tasks allow your app to perform work even when the app is not active or when the device is in the background. React

215

Native provides libraries such as **react-native-background-fetch** to help you execute background tasks like fetching data, sending updates, or syncing data with a server.

1. Installing React Native Background Fetch

To begin, we need to install the **react-native-background-fetch** library, which is used for scheduling background fetch events.

Installation:

bash

npm   install   @transistorsoft/react-native-background-fetch

After installation, make sure to follow the platform-specific instructions for Android and iOS to properly configure the library.

2. Configuring Background Fetch

Once the package is installed and configured, we can set up background task handling. The background fetch event can be triggered periodically to execute certain tasks.

Here's an example of configuring background fetch to call a function in the background:

216

Example: Setting Up Background Fetch

javascript

```javascript
import React, { useEffect } from 'react';
import { View, Text, StyleSheet } from 'react-native';
import BackgroundFetch from '@transistorsoft/react-native-background-fetch';

const BackgroundTaskExample = () => {
  useEffect(() => {
    // Configure the background fetch event
    BackgroundFetch.configure(
      {
        minimumFetchInterval: 15, // Fetch every 15 minutes
        stopOnTerminate: false,    // Continue fetching after app termination
        startOnBoot: true,         // Start fetching after device reboot
        enableHeadless: true,      // Allow background fetch to work in headless mode
      },
      async (taskId) => {
        console.log('[BackgroundFetch] task: ', taskId);
        // Perform background task (e.g., fetching data from API)
```

217

```
      // Example: Fetch data or sync local data
with the server
      try {
        const     response     =     await
fetch('https://api.example.com/sync');
        const data = await response.json();
        console.log('Data synced:', data);
      } catch (error) {
        console.log('Error   fetching   data:',
error);
      }

      // Finish the background task
      BackgroundFetch.finish(taskId);
    },
    (error) => {
      console.log('[BackgroundFetch] failed to
start:', error);
    }
  );

  // Optional:  Configure  events  for  when
background fetch is disabled
  BackgroundFetch.status().then((status) => {
    if              (status              ===
BackgroundFetch.STATUS_DENIED) {
      console.log('Background     fetch     is
denied');
    }
```

```
  });

  return () => {
    // Clean up when component unmounts
    BackgroundFetch.stop();
  };
}, []);

return (
  <View style={styles.container}>
    <Text>Background Task Example</Text>
  </View>
);
};

const styles = StyleSheet.create({
  container: {
    flex: 1,
    justifyContent: 'center',
    alignItems: 'center',
  },
});

export default BackgroundTaskExample;
```

- **Explanation**:
  - o **BackgroundFetch.configure**: This method sets up the background fetch task, specifying how

often it should run (`minimumFetchInterval`) and the tasks to execute in the callback.

- o **Task Handling**: Inside the callback function, you can perform tasks like syncing data with a remote server or performing other background tasks.

- o `BackgroundFetch.finish(taskId)`: This marks the task as complete, allowing the background fetch to stop until the next scheduled run.

- o `enableHeadless`: Enables the background fetch to continue even if the app is terminated.

Sending Local and Push Notifications

Notifications are an important part of mobile apps, allowing you to notify users about updates, reminders, or important events. React Native supports both **local notifications** (for alerts within the app) and **push notifications** (for remote notifications sent from a server).

1. Local Notifications

Local notifications are triggered by your app and can be used to alert users about events within the app.

To send local notifications in React Native, we'll use the **react-native-push-notification** library.

Installation:

```bash
npm install react-native-push-notification
```

After installation, follow the platform-specific setup for iOS and Android.

Example: Sending a Local Notification

```javascript
import React from 'react';
import { View, Button, StyleSheet } from 'react-native';
import PushNotification from 'react-native-push-notification';

const LocalNotificationExample = () => {
  const sendNotification = () => {
    PushNotification.localNotification({
      title: 'Local Notification',
      message: 'This is a local notification!',
      bigText: 'More details about the notification...',
```

221

```
      priority: 'high',    // Priority of the
notification
    });
  };


  return (
    <View style={styles.container}>
      <Button  title="Send  Local  Notification"
onPress={sendNotification} />
    </View>
  );
};


const styles = StyleSheet.create({
  container: {
    flex: 1,
    justifyContent: 'center',
    alignItems: 'center',
  },
});


export default LocalNotificationExample;
```

- **Explanation**:
  - **PushNotification.localNotification** sends a local notification with a title and message.
  - You can also specify additional options like priority, and custom actions for the notification.

2. Push Notifications

Push notifications are sent from a remote server to your app, typically used for things like news updates, reminders, or notifications from other users.

For push notifications, you can use services like **Firebase Cloud Messaging (FCM)** or **OneSignal**.

React Native's `react-native-firebase` library provides seamless integration with Firebase for sending and receiving push notifications.

Installation (for Firebase):

bash

```
npm install --save @react-native-firebase/app
@react-native-firebase/messaging
```

You'll also need to set up Firebase on both iOS and Android. Follow the official React Native Firebase setup guide to complete the installation and configuration.

Example: Receiving Push Notifications with Firebase

javascript

```
import React, { useEffect } from 'react';
```

```
import { View, Text, StyleSheet } from 'react-
native';
import messaging from '@react-native-
firebase/messaging';

const PushNotificationExample = () => {
  useEffect(() => {
    // Request user permission for notifications
    messaging().requestPermission();

    // Foreground notification listener
    const                unsubscribe              =
messaging().onMessage(async remoteMessage => {
      console.log('Foreground          message:',
remoteMessage);
      // Show notification or perform action
based on received message
    });

    // Background/terminated state notification
handler

messaging().onNotificationOpenedApp(remoteMessa
ge => {
      console.log('Notification caused app to
open from background:', remoteMessage);
    });

    return unsubscribe;
```

```
}, []);

return (
  <View style={styles.container}>
    <Text>Push Notification Example</Text>
  </View>
);
};

const styles = StyleSheet.create({
  container: {
    flex: 1,
    justifyContent: 'center',
    alignItems: 'center',
  },
});

export default PushNotificationExample;
```

- **Explanation**:
  - o **messaging().onMessage** listens for push notifications when the app is in the foreground.
  - o **messaging().onNotificationOpenedApp** handles notifications when the app is in the background or terminated.

Real-World Example: Implementing Background Data Sync with Push Notifications

Let's build a real-world example that combines background data synchronization and push notifications. We'll create a simple app that syncs data in the background, and when the sync is completed, the app will send a push notification to the user.

Step 1: Background Sync Task

We'll use the **React Native Background Fetch** library to perform the sync in the background. After the sync completes, we'll send a push notification to the user.

```javascript
import React, { useEffect } from 'react';
import { View, Text, Button, StyleSheet } from
'react-native';
import           BackgroundFetch          from
'@transistorsoft/react-native-background-
fetch';
import PushNotification from 'react-native-push-
notification';

const BackgroundSyncWithNotification = () => {
  useEffect(() => {
    BackgroundFetch.configure(
      {
```

```
        minimumFetchInterval: 15, // Fetch every
15 minutes
        stopOnTerminate: false,      // Continue
after app termination
        startOnBoot: true,               // Start
fetching after device reboot
        enableHeadless: true,        // Headless
mode for background fetch
      },
    async (taskId) => {
      console.log('[BackgroundFetch]   Syncing
data...');

        // Simulate data sync
        setTimeout(() => {
          console.log('[BackgroundFetch]    Data
sync complete!');

          // Send push notification after data
sync
        PushNotification.localNotification({
          title: 'Data Sync',
          message: 'Data sync completed in the
background!',
        });

        BackgroundFetch.finish(taskId);
      }, 3000);
    },
```

```
      (error) => {
        console.log('[BackgroundFetch] failed to
start:', error);
      }
    );

    return () => {
      BackgroundFetch.stop();
    };
  }, []);

  return (
    <View style={styles.container}>
      <Text>Background      Sync      with      Push
Notifications</Text>
    </View>
  );
};

const styles = StyleSheet.create({
  container: {
    flex: 1,
    justifyContent: 'center',
    alignItems: 'center',
  },
});

export default BackgroundSyncWithNotification;
```

- **Explanation**:

o The `BackgroundFetch.configure` method sets up background sync that occurs every 15 minutes.

o After syncing the data, a local push notification is sent to the user to notify them that the sync is complete.

Conclusion

In this chapter, we covered:

- How to manage **background tasks** with **React Native Background Fetch**, allowing tasks like data sync to run in the background.
- How to send **local and push notifications** to inform users about events in your app, even when they are not actively using it.
- A **real-world example** of implementing background data synchronization with push notifications to notify the user once the sync is complete.

Background tasks and notifications are powerful features that can greatly enhance the user experience in your app. In the next chapters, we will explore additional advanced features and techniques to further improve your app's functionality and performance.

CHAPTER 17

TESTING REACT NATIVE APPS

Testing is a critical part of ensuring that your React Native applications are stable, reliable, and perform as expected. By writing effective tests, you can catch bugs early, maintain high-quality code, and improve the developer experience. In this chapter, we will introduce the concepts of **unit testing** and **integration testing**, explore how to write tests for React Native components, actions, and reducers using **Jest**, and walk through a real-world example of writing unit tests for a **login form component**.

Introduction to Unit Testing and Integration Testing with Jest

1. What is Unit Testing?

Unit testing involves testing individual units or components of the application in isolation. In React Native, this typically means testing components, functions, and methods to ensure they behave as expected independently of other parts of the application.

- **Example**: Testing if a function correctly returns the expected output or if a component renders correctly with given props.

2. What is Integration Testing?

Integration testing focuses on testing how different units of the application work together. In React Native, this could involve testing whether multiple components interact correctly, whether data flows between components, or whether external APIs are properly integrated.

- **Example**: Testing if a login component communicates correctly with an authentication API.

3. Jest Overview

Jest is the testing framework that works out-of-the-box with React Native. It provides:

- **Matchers** to check values (e.g., `expect(value).toBe(true)`).
- **Mock functions** to simulate functions or modules.
- **Test runners** to execute tests and provide feedback.

Jest is a powerful tool that can handle both **unit tests** and **integration tests**, making it an excellent choice for testing React Native apps.

232

Installing Jest in a React Native App

Jest is included by default in React Native projects, but you may need to install the necessary testing libraries if they are not set up.

1. Install Jest and React Native Testing Library:

bash

```
npm install --save-dev jest @testing-library/react-native
```

2. Configure Jest in your `package.json` (if not already configured):

json

```
"jest": {
  "preset": "react-native",
  "setupFiles": ["<rootDir>/node_modules/react-native-gesture-handler/jestSetup.js"],
  "transformIgnorePatterns": [
    "node_modules/(?!(react-native|@react-native|react-navigation|@react-navigation)/)"
  ]
}
```

Writing Tests for Components, Actions, and Reducers

1. Writing Tests for Components

React Native components can be tested using Jest and **React Native Testing Library**. Testing components involves rendering the component, simulating user interaction, and asserting the expected outcome.

Example: Testing a Button Component

javascript

```
import React from 'react';
import { render, fireEvent } from '@testing-library/react-native';
import MyButton from './MyButton';

test('button click changes text', () => {
  const { getByText } = render(<MyButton />);
  const button = getByText('Press Me');

  // Simulate button press
  fireEvent.press(button);

  // Check if the button text has changed after press
  expect(getByText('Button Pressed')).toBeTruthy();
});
```

- **Explanation**:
  - o render is used to render the MyButton component.
  - o fireEvent.press simulates a button press.
  - o expect is used to assert that the text changes after the button is pressed.

2. Writing Tests for Actions and Reducers

When testing actions and reducers in Redux, you need to ensure that your actions return the correct type and payload and that reducers return the correct state updates based on the dispatched actions.

Example: Testing an Action

javascript

```
import * as actions from './actions';
import { LOGIN_SUCCESS } from './actionTypes';

test('should create an action to log in', () =>
{
  const user = { username: 'test', password:
'password' };
  const expectedAction = {
    type: LOGIN_SUCCESS,
    payload: user,
  };
```

235

```
expect(actions.loginSuccess(user)).toEqual(expe
ctedAction);
});
```

Example: Testing a Reducer

```javascript
import loginReducer from './loginReducer';
import { LOGIN_SUCCESS } from './actionTypes';

test('should handle LOGIN_SUCCESS', () => {
  const initialState = { user: null, loading:
true };
  const action = { type: LOGIN_SUCCESS, payload:
{ username: 'test' } };
  const expectedState = { user: { username:
'test' }, loading: false };

  expect(loginReducer(initialState,
action)).toEqual(expectedState);
});
```

- **Explanation**:
  - The first test checks if the action creator returns the correct action object.

o The second test checks if the reducer updates the state correctly after the `LOGIN_SUCCESS` action is dispatched.

Real-World Example: Writing Unit Tests for a Login Form Component

Now, let's dive into a **real-world example**. We will write unit tests for a simple **login form component**. This component will contain:

- An input field for the username.
- An input field for the password.
- A submit button that triggers the login process.

We will write tests to ensure that:

1. The input fields are rendered.
2. The submit button triggers the correct behavior.
3. The form validation works correctly.

1. The Login Form Component

LoginForm.js

```javascript
```

237

```
import React, { useState } from 'react';
import { View, TextInput, Button, Text,
StyleSheet } from 'react-native';

const LoginForm = ({ onSubmit }) => {
  const [username, setUsername] = useState('');
  const [password, setPassword] = useState('');
  const [error, setError] = useState('');

  const handleSubmit = () => {
    if (!username || !password) {
      setError('Please fill in both fields');
      return;
    }
    setError('');
    onSubmit(username, password);
  };

  return (
    <View style={styles.container}>
      <TextInput
        placeholder="Username"
        value={username}
        onChangeText={setUsername}
        testID="username-input"
      />
      <TextInput
        placeholder="Password"
        value={password}
```

238

```
        onChangeText={setPassword}
        secureTextEntry
        testID="password-input"
      />
      {error  &&  <Text  testID="error-message"
style={styles.errorText}>{error}</Text>}
      <Button                         title="Login"
onPress={handleSubmit} testID="submit-button" />
    </View>
  );
};


const styles = StyleSheet.create({
  container: {
    flex: 1,
    justifyContent: 'center',
    padding: 20,
  },
  errorText: {
    color: 'red',
    marginBottom: 10,
  },
});


export default LoginForm;
```

- **Explanation**:
  - The LoginForm component manages the state for the username, password, and error message.

239

- o The `handleSubmit` function checks whether both fields are filled out before calling the `onSubmit` prop.
- o We use the `testID` prop to help with selecting elements in our tests.

2. Writing Unit Tests for the Login Form Component

Now, let's write tests for the `LoginForm` component to ensure it behaves as expected.

LoginForm.test.js

javascript

```
import React from 'react';
import { render, fireEvent } from '@testing-
library/react-native';
import LoginForm from './LoginForm';

test('renders the username and password input
fields', () => {
  const { getByTestId } = render(<LoginForm
onSubmit={() => {}} />);

  const usernameInput = getByTestId('username-
input');
  const passwordInput = getByTestId('password-
input');
```

240

```
  expect(usernameInput).toBeTruthy();
  expect(passwordInput).toBeTruthy();
});


test('shows error message when fields are empty
and submit is pressed', () => {
  const   {   getByTestId,   getByText   }   =
render(<LoginForm onSubmit={() => {}} />);

  fireEvent.press(getByTestId('submit-
button'));

  const errorMessage = getByText('Please fill in
both fields');
  expect(errorMessage).toBeTruthy();
});


test('calls onSubmit with correct values when
form is valid', () => {
  const mockSubmit = jest.fn();
  const  {  getByTestId  }  =  render(<LoginForm
onSubmit={mockSubmit} />);

  fireEvent.changeText(getByTestId('username-
input'), 'testuser');
  fireEvent.changeText(getByTestId('password-
input'), 'password123');
```

241

```
    fireEvent.press(getByTestId('submit-
button'));


expect(mockSubmit).toHaveBeenCalledWith('testus
er', 'password123');
});

test('does   not   call   onSubmit   if   fields   are
empty', () => {
    const mockSubmit = jest.fn();
    const  {  getByTestId  }  =  render(<LoginForm
onSubmit={mockSubmit} />);

    fireEvent.press(getByTestId('submit-
button'));

    expect(mockSubmit).not.toHaveBeenCalled();
});
```

- **Explanation**:
  - The first test ensures that both the **username** and **password** input fields are rendered.
  - The second test checks that an error message is shown if the fields are empty when the submit button is pressed.
  - The third test verifies that the onSubmit function is called with the correct values when the form is valid.

242

    o   The fourth test ensures that `onSubmit` is not called if the fields are empty.

Conclusion

In this chapter, we covered how to write **unit tests** and **integration tests** for your React Native apps using **Jest**. We explored:

- **Unit testing components**, actions, and reducers in React Native.
- **Integration testing** for testing how components work together.
- A **real-world example** of writing tests for a **login form component**, including field validation and submit behavior.

By writing thorough tests, you ensure that your app is reliable and maintainable, and it becomes easier to catch bugs early in the development process. In the next chapters, we'll explore further testing strategies, including testing asynchronous actions, mock functions, and UI components in complex scenarios.

Part 5

Building and Deploying

Mobile Apps

CHAPTER 18

PREPARING FOR APP DEPLOYMENT

As your React Native app nears completion, it's time to prepare for deployment. This involves a series of steps to ensure that your app is ready for submission to the **App Store** (iOS) and **Google Play** (Android). In this chapter, we will guide you through the process of setting up your app for both Android and iOS builds, configuring the app for submission, managing assets like app icons and splash screens, and updating metadata.

By the end of this chapter, you will understand the essential steps for preparing your React Native app for submission and be ready to launch your app to a global audience.

Setting Up for Android and iOS Builds

1. Setting Up Android Build

Before you can create an Android build for your React Native app, you need to ensure that you have the correct environment set up. This includes having **Android Studio** installed, along with the appropriate **SDKs** and **JDK** (Java Development Kit).

Steps for Android Build Setup:

1. **Install Android Studio**: Download and install Android Studio from here.

2. **Set up Android SDK**:
   - Open Android Studio and go to **Preferences** > **Appearance & Behavior** > **System Settings** > **Android SDK**.
   - Install the necessary SDK versions, including the latest **Android SDK** and **Android Build Tools**.

3. **Configure Environment Variables**:
   - Set the ANDROID_HOME environment variable to the location of your Android SDK.
   - Add platform-tools and tools directories to your system's PATH.

Building the APK (Android): Once everything is set up, you can build your APK by running the following command in your React Native project directory:

```bash

npx react-native run-android
```

This will generate a debug build and install it on your connected Android device.

To create a release version (a build ready for submission to the Google Play Store), follow these steps:

1. **Generate the Keystore**: Generate a release keystore by running the following command:

```bash
keytool -genkeypair -v -keystore android/app/my-release-key.keystore -keyalg RSA -keysize 2048 -validity 10000 -alias my-key
```

2. **Configure `gradle.properties`**: In android/gradle.properties, add the following lines to reference your keystore:

```properties
MYAPP_RELEASE_STORE_FILE=my-release-key.keystore
MYAPP_RELEASE_KEY_ALIAS=my-key
MYAPP_RELEASE_STORE_PASSWORD=*****
MYAPP_RELEASE_KEY_PASSWORD=*****
```

3. **Build the Release APK**: Run the following command to generate the release APK:

```bash
```

247

```
cd android
./gradlew assembleRelease
```

The APK will be generated in
`android/app/build/outputs/apk/release`.

2. Setting Up iOS Build

For iOS, you'll need to have **Xcode** installed. Xcode provides the necessary tools to build your app for iOS and handle the deployment process.

Steps for iOS Build Setup:

1. **Install Xcode**: Download and install Xcode from the Mac App Store.

2. **Install CocoaPods**:

```bash
sudo gem install cocoapods
```

3. **Install iOS Dependencies**: After installing CocoaPods, navigate to the iOS folder and install the dependencies:

```bash
cd ios
```

248

```
pod install
```

Building the iOS App: Once the environment is set up, you can create a build for iOS:

```
bash
```

```
npx react-native run-ios
```

For a release build, you need to archive the app using Xcode:

1. Open the project in **Xcode** (`ios/YourAppName.xcworkspace`).
2. Select **Generic iOS Device** or your device as the target.
3. Go to **Product** > **Archive** to create an archive of your app.

Once archived, you can submit the app to the **App Store** using **Xcode's Organizer**.

Configuration for App Store and Google Play

1. App Store Configuration (iOS)

To submit your app to the App Store, you need to ensure that the following configurations are correct:

- **App Identifier**: Set your app's unique identifier in the **Apple Developer Center**.

- **Provisioning Profile**: Create an **Ad Hoc** or **App Store** provisioning profile.
- **App Version**: Ensure your app has a version number and build identifier in **Xcode**.
- **App Icons and Splash Screens**: Ensure you have set the appropriate icons and splash screens for different device sizes (more on this below).
- **App Store Connect**: Upload your app to **App Store Connect** using Xcode or **Transporter**.

2. Google Play Configuration (Android)

For Android, you need to configure the following in the **Google Play Console**:

- **App Package Name**: This is the unique identifier for your app, and it should match the one defined in `android/app/build.gradle`.
- **Version Code and Version Name**: Increment the version code for each new release and provide a version name.
- **App Icons**: Set app icons for different screen densities.
- **Sign the APK**: Make sure your APK is signed with your release keystore.
- **Screenshots and Description**: Provide app screenshots, a description, and other metadata for your app listing.

Managing App Icons, Splash Screens, and Metadata

1. App Icons

App icons are an important part of your app's branding. Both iOS and Android require multiple icon sizes for different screen densities.

iOS Icons:

1. Set your **App Icon** in Xcode:
   o Go to **Xcode** > **Assets.xcassets** > **AppIcon**.
   o Add the necessary icon sizes for different device resolutions.

Android Icons:

1. Place your app icon in the following directories within the `android/app/src/main/res` folder:
   o **mdpi**: 48x48 px
   o **hdpi**: 72x72 px
   o **xhdpi**: 96x96 px
   o **xxhdpi**: 144x144 px
   o **xxxhdpi**: 192x192 px

2. Splash Screens

A splash screen is the first screen that appears when the app is launched. Both iOS and Android require splash screens of different sizes.

iOS Splash Screens:

1. Set splash screen images in **LaunchScreen.xib** in Xcode.
2. Define the required image sizes for iPhone and iPad.

Android Splash Screens:

1. Define a splash screen in `android/app/src/main/res/drawable` and `drawable-xxhdpi` folders.
2. You can use libraries like **react-native-splash-screen** to control when the splash screen appears and disappears.

3. Metadata

App metadata includes information such as:

*   **App Name**: The name of your app.
*   **Description**: A short description of your app's functionality.
*   **Keywords**: Keywords for search optimization.

- **Screenshots**: Screenshots for App Store and Google Play listings.
- **Privacy Policy URL**: Required for certain types of apps, such as those that collect personal information.

Real-World Example: Preparing a React Native App for Submission

Let's walk through a real-world scenario of preparing a React Native app for submission to the **App Store** and **Google Play**. In this example, we'll focus on:

- Creating a release build for both Android and iOS.
- Ensuring that app icons, splash screens, and metadata are properly configured.
- Preparing for submission to the respective stores.

Step 1: Configure App Icons and Splash Screens

- Use `react-native-make` or `expo-app-icon` to automatically generate app icons and splash screens for various sizes.

Install react-native-make:

bash

```
npm install -g react-native-make
```

253

- **Generate Icons**:

```bash
react-native set-icon --path ./assets/icon.png
```

- **Generate Splash Screen**:

```bash
react-native set-splash --path ./assets/splash.png
```

Step 2: Build the App

- **Android**: Run `./gradlew assembleRelease` to create a release APK.
- **iOS**: Use Xcode to archive the app and generate an `.ipa` file.

Step 3: Set Up App Metadata

- On the **App Store Connect** (iOS), enter your app's description, keywords, screenshots, and set the version number.
- On **Google Play Console** (Android), provide similar metadata including a description, screenshots, and upload the APK file.

254

Step 4: Submit to the Stores

- **iOS**: Submit the `.ipa` file using **Xcode** or **Transporter**.
- **Android**: Upload the signed `.apk` or `.aab` file to the **Google Play Console**.

Conclusion

In this chapter, we covered the essential steps to prepare your **React Native app** for deployment to the **App Store** and **Google Play**. These steps include:

- Setting up builds for **Android** and **iOS**.
- Configuring **app icons**, **splash screens**, and **metadata**.
- A **real-world example** of preparing a React Native app for submission to both stores.

With these steps completed, your app will be ready for submission to the **App Store** and **Google Play**, and you can begin reaching users around the world. In the next chapters, we'll explore ongoing maintenance, app updates, and additional strategies for app optimization and monitoring after deployment.

CHAPTER 19

CONTINUOUS INTEGRATION AND DELIVERY (CI/CD)

In modern software development, Continuous Integration (CI) and Continuous Delivery (CD) have become essential practices for streamlining the development process, reducing errors, and automating deployment. CI/CD pipelines help teams deliver high-quality code faster and more reliably.

In this chapter, we'll explore how to implement CI/CD for **React Native apps** using popular tools like **Bitrise** and **CircleCI**. We'll go through the steps of setting up automated build and deployment pipelines, ensuring that your React Native app is continuously tested, built, and deployed in a smooth and efficient manner.

Introduction to CI/CD in React Native

What is CI/CD?

- **Continuous Integration (CI)**: The practice of automatically integrating changes into the main codebase frequently, usually multiple times a day. This often includes running automated tests to catch issues early in the development cycle.

- **Continuous Delivery (CD)**: The practice of automatically deploying code to production or staging environments after successful integration and testing. This ensures that new features and bug fixes are available to users as quickly as possible.

CI/CD pipelines provide several benefits:

- **Faster Feedback**: Developers get feedback on their code quickly, catching issues early.
- **Automated Testing**: Helps ensure that all tests pass before code is merged, reducing manual testing and human error.
- **Reliable Deployment**: Automation of the deployment process leads to fewer mistakes and quicker releases.

For **React Native** apps, CI/CD ensures that both the Android and iOS versions of the app are tested, built, and deployed in a streamlined process, reducing the chances of errors during manual deployment.

Setting Up Automated Build and Deployment Pipelines with Services like Bitrise and CircleCI

1. Bitrise Overview

Bitrise is a CI/CD service specifically tailored to mobile app development. It provides pre-built workflows for both Android and iOS apps, making it easy to set up pipelines for React Native apps.

Setting Up Bitrise for React Native

Step 1: Sign Up for Bitrise

1. Go to the Bitrise website and create an account.
2. Once logged in, click on **"Add New App"**.

Step 2: Connect Your Repository

1. Bitrise allows integration with GitHub, GitLab, and Bitbucket. Choose your repository from the connected Git provider.
2. Choose your app type. For React Native, you'll select **"React Native"** from the list of supported project types.

Step 3: Configure the Workflow

1. Bitrise provides an automated workflow configuration. You can start with the default workflow, but you might need to customize it based on your project requirements.

2. Typical steps in the default React Native workflow:

   o **Git Clone Repository**: Clone the repository from GitHub.

   o **Install Dependencies**: Run `npm install` or `yarn install` to install project dependencies.

   o **Install Android/iOS Dependencies**: Run `pod install` for iOS and other necessary steps.

   o **Build APK for Android**: Use Gradle to build the Android APK.

   o **Build IPA for iOS**: Use Xcode to build the IPA file.

   o **Run Tests**: Run unit tests using Jest or other testing libraries.

Step 4: Triggering Builds

- After the workflow is configured, you can set up automatic triggers for your builds. Bitrise can automatically trigger a build whenever a commit is pushed to your repository or a pull request is created.

Step 5: Deploy the App

- Once the build is successful, Bitrise allows you to upload the APK or IPA to app stores or distribute them to testers (via TestFlight for iOS, for example).

2. CircleCI Overview

CircleCI is another popular CI/CD service that is highly customizable. CircleCI integrates with various version control platforms like GitHub and Bitbucket. It provides easy-to-use configuration files to define build, test, and deploy pipelines.

Setting Up CircleCI for React Native

Step 1: Sign Up for CircleCI

1. Create an account on the CircleCI website and link your GitHub or Bitbucket repository.
2. Once logged in, CircleCI will automatically detect your project and offer to set up a configuration file.

Step 2: Create a `.circleci/config.yml` File CircleCI uses a `config.yml` file to define the workflow for your app. This file is placed in the `.circleci` directory in the root of your project.

Here is a sample `config.yml` for a React Native project:

yaml

```
version: 2.1

executors:
  android-executor:
    docker:
      - image: circleci/python:3.7
    working_directory: ~/repo

  ios-executor:
    docker:
      - image: circleci/ruby:2.6
    working_directory: ~/repo

jobs:
  install_dependencies:
    docker:
      - image: circleci/python:3.7
    steps:
      - checkout
      - run:
          name:  Install  Node.js,  Yarn,  and
dependencies
          command: |
            curl                            -sL
https://deb.nodesource.com/setup_14.x | bash -
            apt-get install -y nodejs
            npm install -g yarn
            yarn install
```

```
            cd ios && pod install && cd ..

test:
  docker:
    - image: circleci/python:3.7
  steps:
    - checkout
    - run:
        name: Run tests
        command: yarn test

android_build:
  docker:
    - image: circleci/python:3.7
  steps:
    - checkout
    - run:
        name: Build APK
        command: |
          cd android
          ./gradlew assembleRelease

ios_build:
  docker:
    - image: circleci/ruby:2.6
  steps:
    - checkout
    - run:
        name: Build IPA
```

```
      command: |
        cd ios
        xcodebuild   -scheme   YourAppName
archive                      -archivePath
~/repo/build/YourAppName.xcarchive

workflows:
  version: 2
  build:
    jobs:
      - install_dependencies
      - test
      - android_build:
          requires:
            - install_dependencies
            - test
      - ios_build:
          requires:
            - install_dependencies
            - test
```

Explanation:

- **Executors** define the environments in which the jobs will run (e.g., `android-executor`, `ios-executor`).
- **Jobs** define the steps for installing dependencies, building the APK/IPA, and running tests.

- **Workflows** define the sequence of jobs that will run. In this case, the `android_build` and `ios_build` jobs depend on `install_dependencies` and `test`.

Step 3: Triggering Builds

- Similar to Bitrise, CircleCI can automatically trigger builds whenever a commit is made to the repository or a pull request is created.

Step 4: Deployment

- CircleCI can integrate with Google Play or App Store Connect for deployment. You can use tools like **Fastlane** to automate the upload process.

Real-World Example: Setting Up CI/CD for a React Native Project

Now, let's walk through the steps of setting up CI/CD for a React Native project using **Bitrise** as an example.

Step 1: Create an Account on Bitrise

1. Go to the Bitrise website and create an account.
2. Connect your GitHub or GitLab account to Bitrise.

Step 2: Create a New App on Bitrise

1. Once logged in, click on **"Add New App"**.

2. Choose the repository for your React Native project from GitHub or GitLab.

3. Choose **React Native** as the platform for the app.

Step 3: Configure the Workflow

1. Bitrise will automatically detect your React Native project and create a basic workflow for you.

2. Review and modify the workflow steps, adding additional steps for building the Android APK, building the iOS IPA, and running tests.

Step 4: Set Up Triggers

1. Configure **triggers** so that Bitrise runs builds automatically when changes are pushed to your repository (e.g., when a pull request is made or code is merged).

Step 5: Upload to App Stores

1. Configure Bitrise to upload the generated APK or IPA to **Google Play** or **App Store Connect**.

2. You can use **Fastlane** or other deployment tools to automate this process within the Bitrise pipeline.

Conclusion

In this chapter, we covered the following aspects of setting up CI/CD for **React Native apps**:

- **Continuous Integration (CI)** and **Continuous Delivery (CD)** fundamentals.
- **Setting up automated build and deployment pipelines** with tools like **Bitrise** and **CircleCI**.
- A **real-world example** of setting up CI/CD for a React Native project to automate the build, test, and deployment process.

Implementing CI/CD not only speeds up the development cycle but also improves the quality and reliability of your React Native app. With CI/CD in place, you can be confident that your app is consistently built, tested, and deployed without manual intervention. In the next chapters, we will explore advanced deployment strategies and how to maintain your app after deployment.

CHAPTER 20

PUBLISHING TO GOOGLE PLAY AND APP STORE

Publishing your app to both the **Google Play Store** and the **Apple App Store** is the final step in bringing your React Native app to users worldwide. Both platforms have their unique requirements and processes, so it's important to understand the steps involved to ensure a smooth submission process.

In this chapter, we will guide you through the process of publishing your React Native app to both the **Google Play Store** and the **Apple App Store**, focusing on the following:

- Steps to publish a **React Native app to the Google Play Store**.
- How to publish to the **Apple App Store**, ensuring you meet all their guidelines.
- A **real-world example** of publishing a finished React Native app to both stores.

Steps to Publish a React Native App to the Google Play Store

Publishing to the **Google Play Store** requires you to prepare a few important elements and follow the Google Play Console's process.

1. Prepare Your Android App for Release

Before submitting your React Native app to Google Play, you need to create a **release build** of your app.

1. **Generate a Signed APK or AAB (Android App Bundle)**:
   - Create a **keystore** file (if you haven't already) for signing your app.

   ```bash
   bash
   ```

   ```bash
   keytool -genkeypair -v -keystore
   android/app/my-release-key.keystore
   -keyalg RSA -keysize 2048 -validity
   10000 -alias my-key
   ```

   - Open the `android/app/build.gradle` file and configure your signing information:

   ```gradle
   gradle
   ```

   ```gradle
   signingConfigs {
   ```

```gradle
release {
    storeFile        file("my-release-
key.keystore")
    storePassword "store_password"
    keyAlias "my-key"
    keyPassword "key_password"
  }
}
```

o   Then configure the release build variant:

```gradle
gradle

buildTypes {
  release {
    signingConfig
signingConfigs.release
    minifyEnabled false
    proguardFiles
getDefaultProguardFile('proguard-
android-optimize.txt'),    'proguard-
rules.pro'
  }
}
```

o   **Generate the APK or AAB**: To build the APK:

```bash
bash

cd android
```

269

```
./gradlew assembleRelease
```

Or to build the AAB (recommended for Play Store submission):

```
bash
```

```
./gradlew bundleRelease
```

This will create an APK or AAB file in `android/app/build/outputs/`.

2. **Prepare App Icons and Screenshots**:
   o Create icons of various sizes for different screen densities. You can use tools like **react-native-make** or manually create these icons and place them in the appropriate directories.
   o Take screenshots of your app running on a device, which will be required for the Google Play listing.

2. Create a Google Play Developer Account

To publish your app, you need to have a **Google Play Developer Account**:

- Go to the Google Play Console.
- Pay the one-time registration fee of $25 to create your developer account.

3. Submit Your App to the Google Play Store

1. **Create a New App in the Google Play Console**:
    - Sign in to the Google Play Console and click on **Create Application**.
    - Select the default language and enter the app's title.

2. **Fill Out the App's Metadata**:
    - Add **app description**, **app screenshots**, **category**, and **contact details**.
    - Upload the **app icon** and provide the necessary details like the **content rating** and **pricing**.

3. **Upload Your APK or AAB**:
    - Under the **Release** section, click on **Create Release**.
    - Upload your **signed APK** or **AAB** file.
    - Follow the prompts to complete the release.

4. **Set Up Pricing and Distribution**:
    - Choose whether your app will be **free** or **paid**.
    - Select the countries and regions where you want to distribute the app.

5. **Submit for Review**:
    - Once all the required information is filled out and you're satisfied with the app, click **Save** and then **Review**.
    - After reviewing, click **Submit** to submit the app for Google Play's review process.

271

4. Monitor Your Submission

- After submission, your app will undergo a review process by Google. This typically takes **a few hours to a couple of days**.

- Once approved, the app will be published on the **Google Play Store**.

Publishing to the Apple App Store and Meeting Its Guidelines

Publishing an app to the **Apple App Store** is a more involved process than Android, as Apple enforces strict guidelines to maintain app quality and security.

1. Prepare Your iOS App for Release

Before submitting your app to the App Store, you need to ensure it's ready for deployment:

1. **Create an App Store Distribution Profile**:
   - Log in to the Apple Developer Center.
   - Navigate to **Certificates, Identifiers & Profiles** and create a **distribution certificate**.
   - Create a **Provisioning Profile** for the App Store.
2. **Set the App Version and Build Number**:
   - In Xcode, go to your project's **General Settings** and set the **version number** and **build number**.

272

This is important for updating your app in the future.

3. **App Icons and Splash Screens**:

    o Set your app icons in **Xcode** and ensure you provide all the required icon sizes for iPhone, iPad, and other Apple devices.

    o Make sure you have **splash screens** set up for all screen sizes.

4. **Testing the App**:

    o Ensure that your app works flawlessly by running it in the **Xcode simulator** and on a **physical device**.

    o Perform comprehensive testing to ensure there are no crashes, UI bugs, or broken features.

2. Create an Apple Developer Account

To submit your app, you need an **Apple Developer Program account**:

• Go to the Apple Developer Program and enroll for a $99/year fee.

3. Submit Your App to the App Store

1. **Prepare the App in Xcode**:

    o Open your project in **Xcode** and ensure it's configured for release.

- o Set the appropriate **Deployment Target, Build Configuration**, and **Signing & Capabilities**.

2. **Archive the App**:
   - o In **Xcode**, select **Generic iOS Device** as the target.
   - o Go to **Product** > **Archive**. This creates a build ready for submission.

3. **Upload the App to App Store Connect**:
   - o Once the app is archived, use **Xcode's Organizer** to upload the app to **App Store Connect**.
   - o Follow the prompts to upload the **IPA** file.

4. **Fill Out Metadata on App Store Connect**:
   - o Go to **App Store Connect** and select **My Apps**.
   - o Click the + button to create a new app.
   - o Add the app's name, description, keywords, screenshots, app icon, and other required details.

5. **Submit for Review**:
   - o After uploading the build, you will be prompted to submit your app for review. Apple will check your app for compliance with their **App Store Review Guidelines**.
   - o This review process can take several days.

4. Monitor Your Submission

- Once your app passes the review, you will receive an **email notification** from Apple, and your app will be available on the **App Store**.
- If your app is rejected, you will need to address the issues specified by Apple and resubmit it.

Real-World Example: Publishing a Finished React Native App to Both Stores

Let's walk through the process of publishing a React Native app that has already been built and tested.

Step 1: Generate Release Builds for Android and iOS

1. **Android**: Build the release APK or AAB using `./gradlew assembleRelease` or `./gradlew bundleRelease`.
2. **iOS**: Use Xcode to archive the app and create an IPA file for submission.

Step 2: Prepare App Store and Google Play Metadata

- **App Icons**: Ensure that app icons are properly set for all device sizes.

- **Screenshots**: Take screenshots of your app on various devices.
- **App Descriptions**: Write clear, concise descriptions for the Google Play and App Store listings.
- **Privacy Policy**: Include a privacy policy URL if your app collects personal information.

Step 3: Submit the App

1. **Google Play**: Follow the steps outlined earlier to upload the APK or AAB to the Google Play Console.
2. **App Store**: Upload the IPA file to **App Store Connect** using Xcode's Organizer.

Step 4: Monitor the App Submission

- Keep track of the review process for both stores. Monitor any feedback or rejection details.
- After approval, your app will be available for download by users.

Conclusion

In this chapter, we walked through the essential steps to publish a **React Native app** to the **Google Play Store** and **Apple App Store**. We covered:

- The process of preparing your app for release on both platforms.
- How to configure app metadata, icons, and screenshots.
- The step-by-step process of submitting your app to both stores for review and approval.

By following these guidelines, you can ensure that your app is ready for a smooth launch and distribution to users around the world.

Part 6

Real-World Projects

CHAPTER 21

BUILDING A SIMPLE BLOGGING PLATFORM

In this chapter, we will walk through the process of building a **full-stack blogging platform** using **React Native** for the front-end and **Firebase** for the back-end. This platform will allow users to:

- Create and manage their blog posts.
- Authenticate via Firebase Authentication.
- Add, update, and delete posts (CRUD operations).
- Comment on posts, fostering interaction.

We will focus on integrating the key features necessary for a blogging platform:

- **User authentication**: Login and sign up with Firebase.
- **CRUD operations**: Create, Read, Update, and Delete posts.
- **Comment section**: Allow users to add comments to each blog post.

Building the Back-End with Firebase

Firebase is an excellent choice for building the back-end of a mobile app, especially for a small-scale app like a blogging platform. It provides a real-time database, user authentication, and easy-to-use APIs for handling storage, authentication, and other backend services.

1. Firebase Setup

Before we dive into the app, let's set up Firebase for our project:

1. **Create a Firebase Project**:
   o   Go to the Firebase Console and create a new project.
   o   Add a Firebase project for your app and configure it for both **Android** and **iOS** platforms.
2. **Enable Firebase Authentication**:
   o   In the Firebase Console, go to **Authentication > Sign-in method**.
   o   Enable **Email/Password** sign-in.
3. **Enable Firestore Database**:
   o   Go to **Firestore Database** in the Firebase console and create a Firestore database.
   o   Set the security rules (for development purposes, you can start with open rules):

   json

```
service cloud.firestore {
  match
/databases/{database}/documents {
    match /{document=**} {
      allow read, write: if true;
    }
  }
}
```

4. **Install Firebase SDK**: In your React Native project, install Firebase and the required dependencies:

```bash
npm install @react-native-firebase/app
@react-native-firebase/auth @react-native-
firebase/firestore
```

5. **Configure Firebase in Your React Native App**: Follow the official Firebase setup guide for React Native to configure both **Android** and **iOS**. Make sure to place the correct configuration files (google-services.json for Android and GoogleService-Info.plist for iOS) in the respective directories.

Building the Front-End with React Native

Now that we've set up Firebase, we can start building the front-end of our blogging platform. Let's focus on the core functionality: authentication, CRUD operations for posts, and a comment section.

1. User Authentication (Sign Up and Login)

For authentication, we'll use **Firebase Authentication** with email and password sign-up and login functionality.

SignUpScreen.js:

```javascript
import React, { useState } from 'react';
import { View, TextInput, Button, Text,
StyleSheet } from 'react-native';
import auth from '@react-native-firebase/auth';

const SignUpScreen = ({ navigation }) => {
  const [email, setEmail] = useState('');
  const [password, setPassword] = useState('');
  const [errorMessage, setErrorMessage] =
useState('');

  const handleSignUp = async () => {
    try {
```

```
      await
auth().createUserWithEmailAndPassword(email,
password);
      navigation.navigate('Home');  //  Redirect
to home screen after successful sign-up
   } catch (error) {
      setErrorMessage(error.message);
   }
  };

  return (
    <View style={styles.container}>
      <TextInput
        style={styles.input}
        placeholder="Email"
        value={email}
        onChangeText={setEmail}
      />
      <TextInput
        style={styles.input}
        placeholder="Password"
        secureTextEntry
        value={password}
        onChangeText={setPassword}
      />
      <Button           title="Sign          Up"
onPress={handleSignUp} />
      {errorMessage          &&           <Text
style={styles.errorText}>{errorMessage}</Text>}
```

```
      </View>
    );
};


const styles = StyleSheet.create({
  container: {
    padding: 20,
    flex: 1,
    justifyContent: 'center',
  },
  input: {
    height: 40,
    borderColor: '#ccc',
    borderWidth: 1,
    marginBottom: 15,
    paddingLeft: 10,
  },
  errorText: {
    color: 'red',
    marginTop: 10,
  },
});


export default SignUpScreen;
```

- **Explanation**: This screen allows users to sign up with an email and password. It uses **Firebase Authentication** to create a new user account and navigates to the **Home Screen** on success.

284

LoginScreen.js:

javascript

```
import React, { useState } from 'react';
import { View, TextInput, Button, Text,
StyleSheet } from 'react-native';
import auth from '@react-native-firebase/auth';

const LoginScreen = ({ navigation }) => {
  const [email, setEmail] = useState('');
  const [password, setPassword] = useState('');
  const [errorMessage, setErrorMessage] =
useState('');

  const handleLogin = async () => {
    try {
      await
auth().signInWithEmailAndPassword(email,
password);
      navigation.navigate('Home'); // Redirect
to home screen after successful login
    } catch (error) {
      setErrorMessage(error.message);
    }
  };

  return (
    <View style={styles.container}>
      <TextInput
```

```
      style={styles.input}
      placeholder="Email"
      value={email}
      onChangeText={setEmail}
    />
    <TextInput
      style={styles.input}
      placeholder="Password"
      secureTextEntry
      value={password}
      onChangeText={setPassword}
    />
    <Button                         title="Login"
onPress={handleLogin} />
    {errorMessage          &&           <Text
style={styles.errorText}>{errorMessage}</Text>}
    </View>
  );
};

const styles = StyleSheet.create({
  container: {
    padding: 20,
    flex: 1,
    justifyContent: 'center',
  },
  input: {
    height: 40,
    borderColor: '#ccc',
```

```
    borderWidth: 1,
    marginBottom: 15,
    paddingLeft: 10,
  },
  errorText: {
    color: 'red',
    marginTop: 10,
  },
});
```

```
export default LoginScreen;
```

- **Explanation**: This screen allows users to log in with their email and password using **Firebase Authentication**. After a successful login, users are redirected to the **Home Screen**.

2. CRUD Operations for Posts

For managing blog posts, we will use **Firebase Firestore** to store and retrieve posts. Firestore allows us to create, read, update, and delete documents in real-time.

CreatePostScreen.js:

```
javascript
```

```
import React, { useState } from 'react';
```

```
import { View, TextInput, Button, StyleSheet }
from 'react-native';
import   firestore   from   '@react-native-
firebase/firestore';

const CreatePostScreen = ({ navigation }) => {
  const [title, setTitle] = useState('');
  const [content, setContent] = useState('');

  const handleCreatePost = async () => {
    try {
      await
firestore().collection('posts').add({
        title,
        content,
        createdAt:
firestore.FieldValue.serverTimestamp(),
      });
      navigation.goBack(); // Go back to the home
screen after creating a post
    } catch (error) {
      console.error('Error   creating   post:   ',
error);
    }
  };

  return (
    <View style={styles.container}>
      <TextInput
```

```
      style={styles.input}
      placeholder="Post Title"
      value={title}
      onChangeText={setTitle}
    />
    <TextInput
      style={styles.input}
      placeholder="Post Content"
      value={content}
      onChangeText={setContent}
    />
    <Button         title="Create         Post"
onPress={handleCreatePost} />
    </View>
  );
};

const styles = StyleSheet.create({
  container: {
    padding: 20,
    flex: 1,
    justifyContent: 'center',
  },
  input: {
    height: 40,
    borderColor: '#ccc',
    borderWidth: 1,
    marginBottom: 15,
    paddingLeft: 10,
```

```
  },
});
```

```
export default CreatePostScreen;
```

- **Explanation**: This screen allows users to create a new blog post by entering a **title** and **content**. The post is added to the **Firestore** database with a **timestamp**.

HomeScreen.js (Displaying Posts):

javascript

```javascript
import React, { useState, useEffect } from
'react';
import { View, Text, Button, FlatList, StyleSheet
} from 'react-native';
import    firestore    from    '@react-native-
firebase/firestore';

const HomeScreen = ({ navigation }) => {
  const [posts, setPosts] = useState([]);

  useEffect(() => {
    const unsubscribe = firestore()
      .collection('posts')
      .orderBy('createdAt', 'desc')
      .onSnapshot(snapshot => {
        const postsData = snapshot.docs.map(doc
=> ({
```

```
        id: doc.id,
        ...doc.data(),
      }));
      setPosts(postsData);
    });

    return () => unsubscribe(); // Unsubscribe
when the component unmounts
  }, []);

  return (
    <View style={styles.container}>
      <FlatList
        data={posts}
        keyExtractor={(item) => item.id}
        renderItem={({ item }) => (
          <View style={styles.postItem}>
            <Text
style={styles.title}>{item.title}</Text>
            <Text>{item.content}</Text>
          </View>
        )}
      />
      <Button title="Create Post" onPress={() =>
navigation.navigate('CreatePost')} />
    </View>
  );
};
```

```
const styles = StyleSheet.create({
  container: {
    padding: 20,
  },
  postItem: {
    marginBottom: 20,
  },
  title: {
    fontWeight: 'bold',
  },
});
```

```
export default HomeScreen;
```

- **Explanation**: The **HomeScreen** fetches the list of posts from **Firestore** and displays them in a `FlatList`. Each post shows the **title** and **content**.

3. Comment Section

You can add a comment section under each post by using **Firestore** to store comments associated with each post.

- Similar to posts, you will create a collection for **comments** in Firestore and link comments to specific posts by storing the post's ID.

Conclusion

In this chapter, we built a **full-stack blogging platform** using **React Native** for the front-end and **Firebase** for the back-end. The platform included:

- **User authentication** with Firebase.
- **CRUD operations** for managing blog posts.
- A **comment section** for interacting with posts.

This project demonstrates how to integrate React Native with Firebase to create a fully functional app with real-time data handling, user authentication, and CRUD operations. With Firebase's easy-to-use APIs, we've built a simple, scalable solution for creating a blogging platform that can be expanded with more features in the future.

In the next chapter, we will explore additional features like push notifications, advanced performance optimizations, and app scaling techniques to make your React Native app more robust.

CHAPTER 22

BUILDING AN E-COMMERCE APP

In this chapter, we will build a fully functional **e-commerce app** using **React Native**. The app will allow users to browse products, add items to their shopping cart, and proceed to checkout. We will also integrate popular payment gateways like **Stripe** and **PayPal** to handle payments.

By the end of this chapter, you will have a clear understanding of how to:

- Create a **product listing page** where users can view items.
- Build a **shopping cart** where users can add, remove, and edit items.
- Implement a **checkout process** with payment gateway integrations.

Let's break down the key features and the steps involved.

Creating a Product Listing Page

The product listing page is where users will browse and select items to purchase. In this section, we'll build a simple list of products that users can view and interact with.

1. Setting Up Product Data

For simplicity, we'll hard-code some sample product data. Later, you can connect this to an actual back-end API for real-world applications.

```javascript
const products = [
  { id: '1', name: 'Product 1', price: 29.99,
image: 'https://via.placeholder.com/150' },
  { id: '2', name: 'Product 2', price: 49.99,
image: 'https://via.placeholder.com/150' },
  { id: '3', name: 'Product 3', price: 19.99,
image: 'https://via.placeholder.com/150' },
];
```

2. Product Listing Page (ProductListScreen.js)

This screen will render the list of products, allowing users to click on a product to view its details and add it to the shopping cart.

```javascript
```

```
import React from 'react';
import { View, Text, FlatList, Image,
TouchableOpacity, StyleSheet } from 'react-
native';

const products = [
  { id: '1', name: 'Product 1', price: 29.99,
image: 'https://via.placeholder.com/150' },
  { id: '2', name: 'Product 2', price: 49.99,
image: 'https://via.placeholder.com/150' },
  { id: '3', name: 'Product 3', price: 19.99,
image: 'https://via.placeholder.com/150' },
];

const ProductListScreen = ({ navigation }) => {
  const renderItem = ({ item }) => (
    <View style={styles.productItem}>
      <Image source={{ uri: item.image }}
style={styles.productImage} />
      <Text
style={styles.productName}>{item.name}</Text>
      <Text
style={styles.productPrice}>${item.price}</Text
>
      <TouchableOpacity
        style={styles.addToCartButton}
        onPress={()                       =>
navigation.navigate('ProductDetails', { product:
item })}
```

```
      >
        <Text  style={styles.addToCartText}>View
Details</Text>
      </TouchableOpacity>
    </View>
  );


  return (
    <FlatList
      data={products}
      keyExtractor={(item) => item.id}
      renderItem={renderItem}
    />
  );
};


const styles = StyleSheet.create({
  productItem: {
    padding: 10,
    borderBottomWidth: 1,
    borderColor: '#ddd',
  },
  productImage: {
    width: 150,
    height: 150,
    resizeMode: 'contain',
  },
  productName: {
    fontWeight: 'bold',
```

297

```
    fontSize: 16,
  },
  productPrice: {
    fontSize: 14,
    color: '#888',
  },
  addToCartButton: {
    marginTop: 10,
    backgroundColor: '#4CAF50',
    padding: 10,
    alignItems: 'center',
  },
  addToCartText: {
    color: 'white',
    fontSize: 14,
  },
});


export default ProductListScreen;
```

- **Explanation**:
  - o The FlatList renders the list of products.
  - o Each product displays an image, name, and price, along with a "View Details" button that navigates to the **ProductDetails** screen when clicked.

Creating a Shopping Cart

The shopping cart is where users can review the products they've added before proceeding to checkout. We will allow users to add and remove items from the cart.

1. Shopping Cart State Management

To manage the shopping cart, we'll use **React's useState** hook.

```javascript
import React, { useState } from 'react';
import { View, Text, Button, FlatList, StyleSheet } from 'react-native';

const ShoppingCartScreen = ({ navigation }) => {
  const [cartItems, setCartItems] = useState([]);

  const addItemToCart = (item) => {
    setCartItems((prevItems) => [...prevItems, item]);
  };

  const removeItemFromCart = (id) => {
    setCartItems((prevItems) => prevItems.filter((item) => item.id !== id));
  };
```

299

```
  const handleCheckout = () => {
    navigation.navigate('Checkout', { cartItems
});
  };

  const renderItem = ({ item }) => (
    <View style={styles.cartItem}>
      <Text
style={styles.cartItemName}>{item.name}</Text>
      <Text
style={styles.cartItemPrice}>${item.price}</Tex
t>
      <Button  title="Remove"  onPress={()  =>
removeItemFromCart(item.id)} />
    </View>
  );

  return (
    <View style={styles.container}>
      <FlatList
        data={cartItems}
        renderItem={renderItem}
        keyExtractor={(item) => item.id}
      />
      <Text style={styles.total}>
        Total: ${cartItems.reduce((total, item)
=> total + item.price, 0).toFixed(2)}
      </Text>
```

```
      <Button    title="Proceed    to    Checkout"
onPress={handleCheckout} />
    </View>
  );
};


const styles = StyleSheet.create({
  container: {
    padding: 20,
    flex: 1,
  },
  cartItem: {
    flexDirection: 'row',
    justifyContent: 'space-between',
    padding: 10,
    borderBottomWidth: 1,
    borderColor: '#ddd',
  },
  cartItemName: {
    fontSize: 16,
  },
  cartItemPrice: {
    fontSize: 14,
    color: '#888',
  },
  total: {
    fontSize: 20,
    fontWeight: 'bold',
    marginTop: 10,
```

```
  },
});
```

```
export default ShoppingCartScreen;
```

- **Explanation**:
  - o `useState` is used to manage the state of the shopping cart.
  - o The `addItemToCart` function adds an item to the cart, while `removeItemFromCart` removes it.
  - o The total price of the cart is dynamically calculated.

Implementing the Checkout Process

The checkout process is where users enter their shipping information and make payment.

1. Checkout Screen (CheckoutScreen.js)

In the checkout screen, we'll integrate a payment gateway (Stripe or PayPal) to process payments.

```
javascript
```

```
import React from 'react';
```

```
import { View, Text, Button, StyleSheet } from
'react-native';

const CheckoutScreen = ({ route }) => {
  const { cartItems } = route.params;

  const handlePayment = () => {
    // Integrate Stripe or PayPal payment gateway
here
    alert('Payment Processed!');
  };

  return (
    <View style={styles.container}>
      <Text style={styles.title}>Checkout</Text>
      <Text style={styles.total}>
        Total: ${cartItems.reduce((total, item)
=> total + item.price, 0).toFixed(2)}
      </Text>
      <Button      title="Pay      with      Stripe"
onPress={handlePayment} />
      <Button      title="Pay      with      PayPal"
onPress={handlePayment} />
    </View>
  );
};

const styles = StyleSheet.create({
  container: {
```

```
    padding: 20,
    flex: 1,
  },
  title: {
    fontSize: 24,
    fontWeight: 'bold',
  },
  total: {
    fontSize: 20,
    fontWeight: 'bold',
    marginTop: 10,
  },
});

export default CheckoutScreen;
```

- **Explanation**:
  - This screen displays the total amount and provides two buttons for payment options: **Stripe** and **PayPal**.
  - The handlePayment function is a placeholder, and in a real app, you would integrate the Stripe or PayPal SDK to process payments.

Integrating Payment Gateways

1. Stripe Integration

To integrate **Stripe** in React Native, you will use the **react-native-stripe-sdk**.

- Install Stripe SDK:

```bash
npm install @stripe/stripe-react-native
```

- Follow the Stripe React Native integration guide to set up the **Stripe API keys**, **backend server**, and payment methods (such as **Stripe Elements** or **Stripe Checkout**).

2. PayPal Integration

For **PayPal** integration, use the **react-native-paypal** SDK or a library like **react-native-paypal-lib**.

- Install PayPal SDK:

```bash
npm install react-native-paypal-lib
```

- Set up PayPal's client ID and integrate the payment flow as per the SDK documentation.

Real-World Example: Building a Fully Functional E-commerce App

Let's wrap it up by putting everything together.

1. **App Structure**:
    o **Product Listing**: Display a list of products with options to view details and add them to the cart.
    o **Shopping Cart**: Manage the cart, remove items, and calculate the total.
    o **Checkout**: Process payments via Stripe or PayPal and complete the purchase.
2. **Testing**: Ensure that the cart, checkout, and payment processes work correctly on both Android and iOS devices.
3. **Deployment**: Once the app is fully functional, you can deploy it to the **Google Play Store** and **Apple App Store** using the steps covered in Chapter 20.

Conclusion

In this chapter, we built a simple **e-commerce app** using **React Native** and **Firebase**. The app allows users to:

• Browse products.
• Add items to their shopping cart.

- Checkout and pay using Stripe or PayPal.

We also walked through integrating popular payment gateways, ensuring a smooth transaction process for the user. This app can be expanded further by adding features such as user profiles, order history, and more sophisticated payment options. By following this chapter, you now have the foundation for building full-fledged e-commerce apps with React Native.

CHAPTER 23

BUILDING A SOCIAL MEDIA APP

In this chapter, we will guide you through building a **simple social media app** using **React Native** and **Firebase**. We will focus on creating essential social media features such as:

- **User feed**: Displaying posts from users.
- **Likes and comments**: Allowing users to interact with posts.
- **Notifications**: Alerting users about new interactions.
- **Real-time features**: Using Firebase to manage real-time data.

By the end of this chapter, you will have the necessary skills to build a basic social media app with real-time capabilities using Firebase.

Creating a User Feed, Likes, Comments, and Notifications

1. Setting Up Firebase for Real-time Features

To build the social media app, we will use **Firebase Firestore** for storing posts, comments, likes, and Firebase **Cloud Messaging** for sending notifications. We'll also use **Firebase Authentication** for user management.

Setting Up Firebase

1. **Create Firebase Project**: Go to the Firebase Console and create a new project.
2. **Enable Firebase Services**:
    o **Firestore**: Set up Firestore to store posts, comments, and likes.
    o **Authentication**: Enable **Email/Password** or **Google Authentication** for user login.
    o **Firebase Cloud Messaging (FCM)**: Set up FCM to send notifications.
3. **Install Firebase SDK** in React Native:

bash

```
npm    install    @react-native-firebase/app
@react-native-firebase/auth @react-native-
firebase/firestore            @react-native-
firebase/messaging
```

2. Creating the User Feed

The user feed will display posts in a scrolling list. Users will be able to see posts from other users, with options to like, comment, and view other interactions.

Creating Posts in Firestore: Each post will have a **user ID, post content, timestamp, likes**, and **comments**.

```javascript
import firestore from '@react-native-firebase/firestore';

const addPost = async (userId, content) => {
  try {
    await firestore().collection('posts').add({
      userId,
      content,
      timestamp: firestore.FieldValue.serverTimestamp(),
      likes: 0,
      comments: [],
    });
  } catch (error) {
    console.error("Error adding post: ", error);
  }
};
```

This function adds a new post to the **posts** collection in Firestore.

3. Displaying the User Feed (FeedScreen.js)

The user feed will be a scrollable list of posts. We'll fetch posts from Firestore and display them.

```javascript
import React, { useState, useEffect } from
'react';
import { View, Text, FlatList, TouchableOpacity,
StyleSheet } from 'react-native';
import firestore from '@react-native-
firebase/firestore';

const FeedScreen = () => {
  const [posts, setPosts] = useState([]);

  useEffect(() => {
    const unsubscribe = firestore()
      .collection('posts')
      .orderBy('timestamp', 'desc')
      .onSnapshot(snapshot => {
        const postsData = snapshot.docs.map(doc
=> ({
          id: doc.id,
          ...doc.data(),
        }));
```

311

```
      setPosts(postsData);
    });

  return () => unsubscribe();
}, []);

const renderPost = ({ item }) => (
  <View style={styles.postContainer}>
    <Text
style={styles.postContent}>{item.content}</Text
>
    <Text style={styles.postTimestamp}>
      {item.timestamp                    ?
item.timestamp.toDate().toLocaleString()      :
'Loading...'}
    </Text>
    <View style={styles.actions}>
      <TouchableOpacity
style={styles.likeButton}>
        <Text>Like ({item.likes})</Text>
      </TouchableOpacity>
      <TouchableOpacity
style={styles.commentButton}>
        <Text>Comment</Text>
      </TouchableOpacity>
    </View>
  </View>
);
```

312

```
  return (
    <FlatList
      data={posts}
      keyExtractor={(item) => item.id}
      renderItem={renderPost}
    />
  );
};

const styles = StyleSheet.create({
  postContainer: {
    padding: 10,
    borderBottomWidth: 1,
    borderColor: '#ddd',
  },
  postContent: {
    fontSize: 16,
  },
  postTimestamp: {
    fontSize: 12,
    color: '#888',
  },
  actions: {
    flexDirection: 'row',
    justifyContent: 'space-between',
    marginTop: 10,
  },
  likeButton: {
    backgroundColor: '#4CAF50',
```

```
    padding: 5,
    borderRadius: 5,
  },
  commentButton: {
    backgroundColor: '#2196F3',
    padding: 5,
    borderRadius: 5,
  },
});

export default FeedScreen;
```

- **Explanation**: The **FeedScreen** fetches posts from Firestore using **onSnapshot**, which listens for real-time updates. It displays each post with the option to like and comment.
- When users like a post or add a comment, we'll update Firestore.

4. Implementing Likes and Comments

For likes, we'll increment the like count in Firestore. For comments, we'll allow users to add text comments to a post.

Handling Likes:

```javascript
```

314

```
const likePost = async (postId, currentLikes) =>
{
  try {
    await
firestore().collection('posts').doc(postId).upd
ate({
      likes: currentLikes + 1,
    });
  } catch (error) {
    console.error("Error liking post: ", error);
  }
};
```

Handling Comments:

```javascript
const addComment = async (postId, comment) => {
  try {
    await
firestore().collection('posts').doc(postId).upd
ate({
      comments:
firestore.FieldValue.arrayUnion(comment),
    });
  } catch (error) {
    console.error("Error    adding    comment:    ",
error);
  }
};
```

- **Explanation**: The `likePost` function increments the like count, and `addComment` uses `arrayUnion` to add a comment to the comments array in Firestore.

5. Sending Notifications with Firebase Cloud Messaging

We can send **push notifications** using Firebase Cloud Messaging (FCM). For simplicity, we'll send a notification when someone likes a post.

Setting up FCM:

1. Enable FCM in the Firebase Console.
2. Get the FCM token for the device using the Firebase SDK.

javascript

```
import messaging from '@react-native-
firebase/messaging';

const getFCMToken = async () => {
  const token = await messaging().getToken();
  console.log('FCM Token:', token);
  return token;
};
```

Sending Notifications: We can use Firebase functions or an external service to send notifications when certain actions occur, such as liking a post. For a real-time app, you could trigger notifications when someone interacts with a post, comment, or likes a comment.

Real-World Example: Building a Simple Social Media App with React Native

Now let's put it all together by building a simple, functional social media app.

1. **Authentication**: Users can sign in using Firebase Authentication (either with Google or Email/Password).
2. **User Feed**: Users can see posts created by others and interact with them by liking or commenting.
3. **Push Notifications**: Users receive notifications when there's activity on their posts or comments.
4. **Real-time Updates**: As users like, comment, or create new posts, changes are reflected in real-time on the feed.

App Flow:

1. Users first **sign in** to the app using Firebase Authentication.
2. After signing in, they can **view the user feed** where they can scroll through posts.
3. They can **like** posts, **comment** on posts, and see **real-time updates**.

4. **Push notifications** are triggered when there is a new interaction, such as a comment or like on their posts.

Conclusion

In this chapter, we built a basic **social media app** using **React Native** and **Firebase**. We covered:

- **User authentication** using Firebase.
- Building a **user feed** where users can view, like, and comment on posts.
- Implementing **real-time features** with Firestore.
- **Push notifications** using Firebase Cloud Messaging (FCM).

This app can be expanded with more advanced features such as user profiles, follow/unfollow functionality, chat systems, and more complex notification handling.

In the next chapter, we will explore more advanced topics such as performance optimization and scaling your social media app for larger audiences.

CHAPTER 24

BUILDING A FITNESS TRACKING APP

In this chapter, we will build a **fitness tracking app** using **React Native**. The app will include key features such as:

- **GPS tracking** for recording user location and distance during workouts.
- **Step counting** to track daily physical activity.
- **Workout logs** to store users' workout sessions and track their progress.
- Integration with external **fitness APIs** and handling **data persistence**.

By the end of this chapter, you will have a functional fitness tracker app with real-time features, data storage, and integration with third-party services.

Implementing GPS Tracking, Step Counting, and Workout Logs

1. GPS Tracking

GPS tracking is an essential feature for a fitness app, allowing users to track their route, distance, and location during outdoor activities such as running, walking, or cycling.

We will use **react-native-location** to get the user's GPS coordinates.

Installation:

bash

npm install react-native-location

Example: Getting GPS Coordinates (TrackingLocation.js)

javascript

```
import React, { useState, useEffect } from
'react';
import { View, Text, Button, StyleSheet } from
'react-native';
import Location from 'react-native-location';

const TrackingLocation = () => {
  const [location, setLocation] =
useState(null);
```

320

```
const    [isTracking,    setIsTracking]    =
useState(false);

  useEffect(() => {
    // Initialize location
    Location.configure({
      distanceFilter: 10, // meters
      enableHighAccuracy: true,
    });

    return () => {
      Location.stop();
    };
  }, []);

  const startTracking = async () => {
    setIsTracking(true);

Location.subscribeToLocationUpdates((locations)
=> {
      setLocation(locations[0]);
    });
  };

  const stopTracking = () => {
    setIsTracking(false);
    Location.stop();
  };
```

```
  return (
    <View style={styles.container}>
      <Text               style={styles.title}>GPS
Tracking</Text>
        {location && (
          <Text style={styles.locationText}>
            Latitude:    {location.latitude}    |
Longitude: {location.longitude}
          </Text>
        )}
        <Button
          title={isTracking ? 'Stop  Tracking'  :
'Start Tracking'}
          onPress={isTracking  ?  stopTracking  :
startTracking}
        />
    </View>
  );
};

const styles = StyleSheet.create({
  container: {
    padding: 20,
    flex: 1,
    justifyContent: 'center',
    alignItems: 'center',
  },
  title: {
    fontSize: 24,
```

```
    marginBottom: 20,
  },
  locationText: {
    fontSize: 18,
    marginBottom: 20,
  },
});
```

```
export default TrackingLocation;
```

- **Explanation**:
  - The `Location` library is used to get the user's current GPS coordinates.
  - The app starts and stops GPS tracking based on the button press. The location updates every 10 meters by default.
  - The app displays the user's latitude and longitude in real-time while tracking.

2. Step Counting

Step counting is an important feature in fitness apps, tracking daily physical activity based on the user's steps.

We can use **react-native-pedometer** to access the step count functionality.

Installation:

```bash
bash

npm install @react-native-community/pedometer
```

Example: Step Counter (StepCounter.js)

```javascript
javascript

import React, { useState, useEffect } from
'react';
import { View, Text, Button, StyleSheet } from
'react-native';
import { Pedometer } from '@react-native-
community/pedometer';

const StepCounter = () => {
  const [stepCount, setStepCount] = useState(0);

  useEffect(() => {
    const startStepCounting = () => {
      Pedometer.startPedometerUpdates((result)
=> {
        setStepCount(result.steps);
      });
    };

    startStepCounting();

    return () => {
      Pedometer.stopPedometerUpdates();
```

324

```
    };
  }, []);

  return (
    <View style={styles.container}>
      <Text              style={styles.title}>Step
Counter</Text>
      <Text   style={styles.stepCountText}>Steps:
{stepCount}</Text>
    </View>
  );
};

const styles = StyleSheet.create({
  container: {
    padding: 20,
    flex: 1,
    justifyContent: 'center',
    alignItems: 'center',
  },
  title: {
    fontSize: 24,
    marginBottom: 20,
  },
  stepCountText: {
    fontSize: 18,
  },
});
```

```
export default StepCounter;
```

- **Explanation**:
  - o **react-native-pedometer** is used to get real-time step count updates from the device's pedometer.
  - o The `startPedometerUpdates` method starts tracking the number of steps, and the `stopPedometerUpdates` method stops it when the component unmounts.

3. Workout Logs

Users need to track their workout activities, such as the type of workout, duration, calories burned, and other metrics. We can store this information in **Firebase Firestore**.

Example: Adding Workout Log (WorkoutLog.js)

```javascript
import React, { useState } from 'react';
import { View, Text, TextInput, Button,
StyleSheet } from 'react-native';
import firestore from '@react-native-
firebase/firestore';

const WorkoutLog = () => {
  const [workoutType, setWorkoutType] =
useState('');
```

```
const [duration, setDuration] = useState('');
const [calories, setCalories] = useState('');

const handleSaveWorkout = async () => {
  try {
    await
firestore().collection('workouts').add({
      workoutType,
      duration,
      calories,
      timestamp:
firestore.FieldValue.serverTimestamp(),
    });
    alert('Workout saved successfully!');
    setWorkoutType('');
    setDuration('');
    setCalories('');
  } catch (error) {
    console.error('Error  saving  workout:  ',
error);
  }
};

return (
  <View style={styles.container}>
    <Text    style={styles.title}>Log    Your
Workout</Text>
    <TextInput
      style={styles.input}
```

```
        placeholder="Workout       Type       (e.g.,
Running)"
        value={workoutType}
        onChangeText={setWorkoutType}
      />
      <TextInput
        style={styles.input}
        placeholder="Duration (minutes)"
        value={duration}
        onChangeText={setDuration}
        keyboardType="numeric"
      />
      <TextInput
        style={styles.input}
        placeholder="Calories Burned"
        value={calories}
        onChangeText={setCalories}
        keyboardType="numeric"
      />
      <Button        title="Save        Workout"
onPress={handleSaveWorkout} />
    </View>
  );
};

const styles = StyleSheet.create({
  container: {
    padding: 20,
    flex: 1,
```

```
    justifyContent: 'center',
  },
  title: {
    fontSize: 24,
    marginBottom: 20,
  },
  input: {
    height: 40,
    borderColor: '#ccc',
    borderWidth: 1,
    marginBottom: 15,
    paddingLeft: 10,
  },
});


export default WorkoutLog;
```

- **Explanation**:
  - The **WorkoutLog** screen allows users to input workout details, such as the type, duration, and calories burned.
  - The workout data is stored in Firestore under the **workouts** collection, with a timestamp for tracking.

Integrating with Fitness APIs and Handling Data Persistence

1. Integrating Fitness APIs

Fitness apps often need to integrate with external fitness services or APIs for advanced data processing and tracking. We'll use **Google Fit API** or **Apple HealthKit** for this purpose. However, for simplicity, we focus on **Firebase** as a backend service, where we can store and retrieve workout data, steps, and location.

2. Handling Data Persistence with Firestore

For persistent storage, we're using **Firebase Firestore** to store user workouts and other fitness data. Firebase provides real-time synchronization, allowing users to access their workout logs across devices.

- Store workout logs, location data, and step counts in **Firestore** for long-term persistence.
- Use **Firebase Authentication** to track workouts per user, ensuring that each user has their own unique workout history.

Real-World Example: Building a Personal Fitness Tracker App

Now, let's put everything together and build a **personal fitness tracker app** that includes:

1. **GPS tracking** for outdoor workouts (like running or cycling).
2. **Step counting** for daily activity tracking.
3. **Workout logs** for storing workout details and tracking progress.

The app will have the following screens:

- **Home Screen**: Displaying GPS tracking, step count, and workout options.
- **Workout Log Screen**: Allowing users to log their workouts and store them in Firebase.
- **Tracking Screen**: Displaying live GPS coordinates, distance, and speed.
- **History Screen**: Showing a list of all past workouts.

Conclusion

In this chapter, we built a **fitness tracking app** using **React Native** and **Firebase**. The app tracks key fitness metrics such as:

- **GPS location** and **distance** during workouts.
- **Step count** for daily activity tracking.
- **Workout logs** for tracking workout sessions.

We used **Firebase Firestore** for data persistence and real-time updates, and we integrated third-party libraries like **react-native-location** and **react-native-pedometer** for GPS tracking and step counting. This app can be further enhanced by integrating with fitness APIs such as **Google Fit** or **Apple HealthKit**, and adding features like workout goals, progress tracking, and social sharing.

In the next chapter, we will explore additional features, performance optimizations, and scaling strategies for fitness apps.

Part 7

Advanced Topics in React Native

CHAPTER 25

REACT NATIVE FOR WEB

React Native, primarily designed for building mobile applications, has evolved to support **web applications** as well. With **React Native for Web**, you can use the same codebase for building apps that work across **iOS**, **Android**, and **web** platforms, greatly improving your app's reach and maintainability. In this chapter, we'll walk you through the process of using **React Native components** to build **web applications** and setting up a **universal React Native project** that targets both mobile and web platforms.

By the end of this chapter, you will be able to:

- Use **React Native components** to create web applications.
- Set up a **universal React Native project** that can run on mobile and web platforms.
- Convert an existing React Native app into a **React Native Web** app.

Using React Native Components to Build Web Applications

React Native components are designed to work across both **mobile** (iOS and Android) and **web**. By leveraging **React Native**

334

for Web, you can reuse the same components and business logic across all platforms.

1. What is React Native for Web?

React Native for Web is a library that enables React Native components and APIs to work on the web. It allows you to write components in **React Native** and render them using **HTML and CSS** on the web. Essentially, you get the same experience, reusing your codebase across mobile and web applications.

- **Core Benefits**:
  - **Code Reusability**: You can share code between web, iOS, and Android.
  - **Consistency**: Ensures the same UI and behavior across platforms.
  - **Efficient Development**: Decreases the development time for multi-platform apps.

2. Setting Up React Native for Web in Your Project

To set up a **React Native for Web** project, you need to install the required dependencies and configure your project to support web, mobile, and other platforms.

Step 1: Install Dependencies

1. First, install `react-native-web`, along with some other necessary packages like `react-dom` and `react-scripts` for the web environment:

bash

```
npm install react-native-web react-dom react-scripts
```

2. Install **react-native** and **react-navigation** dependencies for building mobile apps:

bash

```
npm install react-native react-navigation react-navigation-stack
```

Step 2: Configure Your Project for Web

You'll need to update your project's entry point and webpack configuration to make it work for the web. Below is a basic setup for creating a universal React Native project that works on both mobile and web.

1. Create a new entry point for the web. For example, in the root of your project, create a new file called `index.web.js`:

javascript

```
import { AppRegistry } from 'react-native';
import App from './App';
import { name as appName } from './app.json';
import { BrowserRouter as Router } from 'react-
router-dom';

AppRegistry.registerComponent(appName, () =>
App);
AppRegistry.runApplication(appName, {
  initialProps: {},
  rootTag: document.getElementById('app-root'),
});
```

2. Set up **Webpack** (or use Create React App if starting from scratch) to handle React Native components. Add the necessary loaders and configurations for bundling.

Step 3: Update `App.js` to Work Across Platforms

To ensure your app works on both mobile and web, use **Platform-specific code** to differentiate between web and mobile platforms.

Example:

```javascript

import React from 'react';
import { View, Text, Platform } from 'react-
native';
```

```
const App = () => {
  return (
    <View>
      <Text>
        {Platform.OS === 'web' ? 'Web version of
the app' : 'Mobile version of the app'}
      </Text>
    </View>
  );
};

export default App;
```

- **Explanation**: The `Platform.OS` checks if the app is running on the web or mobile, and displays different text accordingly.

Setting Up a Universal React Native Project for Mobile and Web Platforms

Now that we have installed the necessary packages and configured the entry point for the web, we can set up a **universal React Native project** that supports both mobile and web platforms using **React Native for Web**.

338

1. Creating the Universal Project Structure

The directory structure will look like this:

```bash
/project-root
  /src
    /components
      Button.js
    App.js
  /index.web.js
  /index.js (for mobile)
  /package.json
  /webpack.config.js (for web bundling)
  /metro.config.js (for React Native bundling)
```

2. Setting Up Webpack for Web Build

React Native for Web requires you to set up **Webpack** for bundling your app for the web. You can create a basic webpack.config.js file to get started.

```javascript
const path = require('path');

module.exports = {
  entry: './index.web.js',
  output: {
```

```
    path: path.resolve(__dirname, 'build'),
    filename: 'bundle.js',
  },
  resolve: {
    alias: {
      'react-native$': 'react-native-web',
    },
  },
  module: {
    rules: [
      {
        test: /\.js$/,
        exclude: /node_modules/,
        use: 'babel-loader',
      },
      {
        test: /\.css$/,
        use: ['style-loader', 'css-loader'],
      },
    ],
  },
  devServer: {
    contentBase: path.join(__dirname, 'public'),
    compress: true,
    port: 3000,
  },
};
```

- **Explanation**: This configuration sets up **Webpack** to resolve React Native components to their web equivalents using **react-native-web**. It also configures Babel to transpile JavaScript and adds support for CSS.

3. Using Platform-Specific Code in Components

To optimize your app for both web and mobile, you can use **Platform-specific code** to create components that render differently based on the platform.

For example, if you have a custom button component, you can write platform-specific versions:

Button.js (Universal Component)

javascript

```javascript
import React from 'react';
import { Button as RNButton, Platform, Text }
from 'react-native';

const Button = ({ title, onPress }) => {
  if (Platform.OS === 'web') {
    return (
      <button onClick={onPress}>
        <Text>{title}</Text>
      </button>
    );
```

341

```
}
```

```
return          <RNButton          title={title}
onPress={onPress} />;
};
```

```
export default Button;
```

- **Explanation**: The `Button` component renders a `<button>` element on the web, but uses the native `Button` component for mobile platforms.

Real-World Example: Converting a React Native App to a React Native Web App

Let's take a simple **React Native mobile app** and convert it into a **React Native Web app**.

Step 1: Set Up the Project

1. Create a new **React Native project**:

   bash

   ```
   npx react-native init UniversalApp
   ```

2. Install **React Native Web**:

```bash
bash
```

```
npm install react-native-web react-dom
react-scripts
```

Step 2: Update App.js

Make sure that your main component, App.js, uses **Platform-specific code** and works across web and mobile:

```javascript
javascript

import React from 'react';
import { View, Text, Button, Platform } from
'react-native';
import { AppRegistry } from 'react-native';

const App = () => {
  return (
    <View style={{ padding: 20 }}>
      <Text>Welcome to the Universal App!</Text>
      {Platform.OS === 'web' ? (
        <button onClick={() => alert('Web Button
Clicked')}>Web Button</button>
      ) : (
        <Button title="Mobile Button"
onPress={() => alert('Mobile Button Clicked')} />
      )}
    </View>
  );
```

```
};

AppRegistry.registerComponent('UniversalApp', ()
=> App);
AppRegistry.runApplication('UniversalApp', {
  initialProps: {},
  rootTag: document.getElementById('app-root'),
});

export default App;
```

- **Explanation**: The app displays a **different button** based on the platform. If the app is running on the web, a `<button>` is displayed; otherwise, the native `Button` component is used for mobile.

Step 3: Set Up Webpack and Metro Config

Follow the earlier instructions to set up **Webpack** and **Metro bundler** for React Native. This configuration ensures that the app works seamlessly on both mobile and web.

Step 4: Run the Web App

After setting up the **webpack.config.js** and **index.web.js**, run the web app using:

```bash
bash
```

```
npm run start
```

This will open the app in the browser using **React Native for Web**.

Conclusion

In this chapter, we explored the concept of **React Native for Web**, which enables you to build cross-platform apps for mobile and web using the same codebase. We covered:

- How to set up a **universal React Native project** that targets both **web** and **mobile** platforms.
- How to use **React Native components** to create web applications.
- How to handle **platform-specific code** to render components differently on web and mobile.

With **React Native for Web**, you can expand your app's reach to multiple platforms and maintain a single codebase, improving development efficiency and user experience. In the next chapter, we will explore more advanced features like code splitting, performance optimizations, and deploying a universal app to production.

CHAPTER 26

STATE MANAGEMENT IN REACT NATIVE WITH REDUX

In this chapter, we will explore **state management** in React Native using **Redux**, one of the most popular state management libraries for JavaScript applications. Redux allows you to manage the state of your app in a predictable way, making it easier to track and update data across multiple components.

We will cover:

- **Introduction to Redux**: How Redux works and why it's useful.
- **Managing app state with Redux**: Integrating Redux with React Native to manage the state of your app.
- **Real-world example**: Building a **shopping cart app** with Redux to demonstrate how to handle state in a complex application.

By the end of this chapter, you will have a solid understanding of how to use Redux for state management in your React Native apps and how to integrate it with your components.

Introduction to Redux and How It Works

1. What is Redux?

Redux is a **state management library** that helps you manage and centralize the state of your application. It is based on the idea of a **single store** that holds the entire application state, and components can **dispatch actions** to modify this state.

Redux follows a strict flow:

- **Actions**: Describe the changes to be made to the state.
- **Reducers**: Specify how the state should change in response to actions.
- **Store**: Holds the state of the application.
- **Dispatch**: Sends actions to the reducer to update the store.

2. Key Concepts in Redux

- **Store**: A central repository of the application state.
- **Action**: A plain JavaScript object that describes an event or a change in the state.
- **Reducer**: A function that accepts the current state and an action and returns a new state.
- **Dispatch**: A method used to send an action to the reducer to update the state.

3. Why Use Redux in React Native?

In a React Native app, you may have multiple components that need to share and update the same state. Without Redux, managing state across these components can become cumbersome. Redux provides:

- A **single source of truth** for the state.
- **Predictable state transitions**, making it easier to track changes.
- An easy way to **share data** between components.

Managing App State with Redux and Connecting It to React Native Components

1. Setting Up Redux in a React Native Project

To start using Redux, we first need to install the necessary packages:

bash

```
npm install redux react-redux
```

- **redux**: The core library that implements the Redux functionality.
- **react-redux**: The official library that helps connect Redux with React (or React Native) components.

348

2. Creating Redux Store and Reducer

The first step in setting up Redux is creating a **store** and a **reducer**.

Creating the Reducer (cartReducer.js):

A reducer is a pure function that takes the current state and an action, and returns a new state.

```javascript
// cartReducer.js

const initialState = {
  cartItems: [],
};

const cartReducer = (state = initialState,
action) => {
  switch (action.type) {
    case 'ADD_ITEM':
      return {
        ...state,
        cartItems:         [...state.cartItems,
action.payload],
      };
    case 'REMOVE_ITEM':
      return {
        ...state,
```

349

```
        cartItems:    state.cartItems.filter(item
=> item.id !== action.payload.id),
      };
    default:
      return state;
  }
};
```

```
export default cartReducer;
```

- **Explanation**: The `cartReducer` manages the state of the shopping cart. It handles actions like adding and removing items from the cart.

Creating the Store (store.js):

The **store** holds the entire state of the app. You create a store by passing your root reducer to the Redux `createStore` function.

```
javascript
```

```javascript
// store.js

import { createStore } from 'redux';
import cartReducer from './cartReducer';

const store = createStore(cartReducer);

export default store;
```

- **Explanation**: We create a store with `createStore` and pass it the `cartReducer` to manage the state of the shopping cart.

3. Connecting Redux to React Native Components

Now that we have set up the store and the reducer, we need to **connect Redux** to our React Native components using the `react-redux` library.

Using the Provider (App.js):

The `Provider` component makes the Redux store available to all components in the app.

javascript

```
// App.js

import React from 'react';
import { View, Text, Button } from 'react-
native';
import { Provider } from 'react-redux';
import store from './store';
import CartScreen from './CartScreen';

const App = () => {
  return (
    <Provider store={store}>
```

```
    <View style={{ flex: 1 }}>
      <CartScreen />
    </View>
  </Provider>
 );
};
```

```
export default App;
```

- **Explanation**: We wrap our entire app in the `Provider` component and pass the Redux `store` to it. This makes the Redux store accessible to all components within the app.

4. Dispatching Actions in Components

Now let's connect the `CartScreen` component to Redux. We will display the list of cart items and allow users to add or remove items using actions.

CartScreen.js:

javascript

```
// CartScreen.js

import React from 'react';
import { View, Text, Button, FlatList, StyleSheet
} from 'react-native';
```

```
import { connect } from 'react-redux';


const CartScreen = ({ cartItems, addItem,
removeItem }) => {
  const renderItem = ({ item }) => (
    <View style={styles.item}>
      <Text>{item.name} - ${item.price}</Text>
      <Button title="Remove" onPress={()   =>
removeItem(item)} />
    </View>
  );


  return (
    <View style={styles.container}>
      <Text          style={styles.title}>Shopping
Cart</Text>
      <FlatList
        data={cartItems}
        keyExtractor={(item)                 =>
item.id.toString()}
        renderItem={renderItem}
      />
      <Button
        title="Add Random Item"
        onPress={()     =>     addItem({    id:
Math.random(),    name:    'Product',    price:
Math.floor(Math.random() * 100) })}
      />
    </View>
```

```
  );
};


const styles = StyleSheet.create({
  container: {
    flex: 1,
    padding: 20,
  },
  title: {
    fontSize: 24,
    fontWeight: 'bold',
  },
  item: {
    marginVertical: 10,
  },
});


const mapStateToProps = (state) => ({
  cartItems: state.cartItems,
});


const mapDispatchToProps = (dispatch) => ({
  addItem: (item) => dispatch({ type: 'ADD_ITEM',
payload: item }),
  removeItem:  (item)  =>  dispatch({  type:
'REMOVE_ITEM', payload: item }),
});
```

```
export     default     connect(mapStateToProps,
mapDispatchToProps)(CartScreen);
```

- **Explanation**:
  - o The `CartScreen` component is connected to Redux using the `connect` function from `react-redux`.
  - o `mapStateToProps` maps the state (cartItems) from Redux to the component's props.
  - o `mapDispatchToProps` maps the dispatch of actions (`addItem` and `removeItem`) to the component's props.
  - o The `addItem` and `removeItem` actions are dispatched to update the Redux store.

Real-World Example: Building a Shopping Cart App with Redux

Now that we've seen how Redux works with React Native, let's walk through building a simple **shopping cart app** using Redux to manage the cart items.

1. **Set up Redux Store**: Create a store with `createStore`, and manage the shopping cart state (items added, removed).

355

2. **Dispatch Actions**: Use `dispatch` to add or remove items from the cart by calling Redux actions from components.

3. **Connecting Components**: Use `connect` to connect React Native components (like `CartScreen`) to the Redux store, so the state is automatically updated when items are added or removed.

Final Structure of the Shopping Cart App:

- **Redux**: Manages the shopping cart state (cartItems) and provides actions to update the cart.
- **CartScreen**: Displays the list of items in the cart, with options to add or remove items.
- **App.js**: Wraps the app in a `Provider` to make the Redux store available to all components.

Conclusion

In this chapter, we covered how to manage state in **React Native** using **Redux**:

- We learned the basic concepts of Redux: **actions**, **reducers**, and the **store**.
- We set up a **Redux store** to manage the shopping cart state.

- We integrated **Redux** with React Native components using the `connect` function from **react-redux** to dispatch actions and access state.

The **shopping cart app** we built is a simple example of how Redux can be used to manage state in a React Native app. You can extend this app with more features, such as user authentication, checkout flow, and integration with a back-end API.

Redux is a powerful tool for managing state in large, complex applications, and it is widely used in production apps. In the next chapter, we will explore more advanced topics in Redux, such as middleware, asynchronous actions, and optimization techniques.

CHAPTER 27

ADVANCED NATIVE INTEGRATION AND NATIVE UI COMPONENTS

In this chapter, we will delve into **advanced native integration in React Native**. React Native offers a high degree of flexibility, enabling developers to extend their app with **custom native modules** and integrate **native UI components** for enhanced performance and functionality. By creating and using these native components, you can access platform-specific features and offer users a smoother, more powerful app experience.

We will explore:

- **Extending React Native** with advanced **native modules** and **custom views**.
- **Integrating complex native UI components** into a React Native app.
- A **real-world example**: Integrating a **custom native camera module** for image processing, including capturing images and applying transformations.

Extending React Native with Advanced Native Modules and Custom Views

1. What Are Native Modules?

Native modules are pieces of code that are written in **Java**, **Objective-C**, **Swift**, or **Objective-C++**, and allow you to access platform-specific APIs that are not available in JavaScript. React Native bridges the gap between JavaScript and the native platform, enabling your app to interact with native features.

- **Native Modules** are used when you need functionality not covered by the React Native APIs.
- **Custom Views** are UI components created natively that are embedded into React Native. These are useful when you need a custom, platform-specific UI element.

2. Creating a Native Module

To create a native module, you need to write platform-specific code that interacts with the JavaScript side using a **bridge**. The bridge allows JavaScript to invoke native functionality.

Here's a basic workflow for creating a native module in **React Native**:

- **Step 1**: Create the native code.
- **Step 2**: Create the JavaScript interface to access that native code.

359

- **Step 3**: Expose the functionality from the native code to JavaScript using the React Native bridge.

Example: Creating a Custom Native Camera Module

Let's walk through the process of creating a custom native camera module that can capture an image and return it to the React Native app.

Step 1: Create the Native Code (Android and iOS)

For Android: You'll need to create a native Android module to interact with the device's camera.

1. Open your Android project in **Android Studio**.
2. In the **android/app/src/main/java/com/yourapp** directory, create a new Java class (e.g., CustomCameraModule.java).

```java
java

package com.yourapp;

import android.app.Activity;
import android.content.Intent;
import android.provider.MediaStore;
import android.util.Log;
```

```
import
com.facebook.react.bridge.ReactApplicationConte
xt;
import
com.facebook.react.bridge.ReactContextBaseJavaM
odule;
import com.facebook.react.bridge.ReactMethod;
import com.facebook.react.bridge.Callback;

public    class    CustomCameraModule    extends
ReactContextBaseJavaModule {

    public
CustomCameraModule(ReactApplicationContext
reactContext) {
        super(reactContext);
    }

    @Override
    public String getName() {
        return "CustomCamera";
    }

    @ReactMethod
    public          void          openCamera(Callback
successCallback, Callback errorCallback) {
        try {
            Activity        currentActivity        =
getCurrentActivity();
```

```
        if (currentActivity != null) {
            Intent    intent    =    new
Intent(MediaStore.ACTION_IMAGE_CAPTURE);

currentActivity.startActivityForResult(intent,
1);
                successCallback.invoke("Camera
opened successfully.");
            } else {
                errorCallback.invoke("Unable  to
open camera.");
            }
        } catch (Exception e) {
            errorCallback.invoke("Error  opening
camera: " + e.getMessage());
        }
    }
}
```

- **Explanation**: The `CustomCameraModule` opens the camera using Android's `MediaStore.ACTION_IMAGE_CAPTURE` intent. The `openCamera` method is exposed to JavaScript through the React Native bridge.

For iOS: You will create a similar native module in **Objective-C** or **Swift**. For simplicity, here's an example using **Objective-C**.

1. Open your iOS project in **Xcode**.

362

2. In the **ios/YourApp** directory, create a new Objective-C class (e.g., CustomCameraModule.m).

objc

```objc
#import <React/RCTBridgeModule.h>
#import <UIKit/UIKit.h>

@interface    CustomCameraModule    :    NSObject
<RCTBridgeModule>
@end

@implementation CustomCameraModule

RCT_EXPORT_MODULE();

RCT_EXPORT_METHOD(openCamera:(RCTResponseSender
Block)successCallback

errorCallback:(RCTResponseSenderBlock)errorCall
back) {
  UIImagePickerController      *picker      =
[[UIImagePickerController alloc] init];
  picker.sourceType                          =
UIImagePickerControllerSourceTypeCamera;

  UIViewController    *currentViewController    =
[UIApplication
```

363

```
sharedApplication].keyWindow.rootViewController
;

  [currentViewController
presentViewController:picker        animated:YES
completion:nil];

  successCallback(@[@"Camera          opened
successfully."]);
}
```

```
@end
```

- **Explanation**: The `CustomCameraModule` opens the camera on iOS. The `openCamera` method is exposed to JavaScript through the React Native bridge, using `RCT_EXPORT_METHOD`.

Step 2: Create the JavaScript Interface

Now, on the JavaScript side, you will create a wrapper for the native module to expose it to React Native components.

CustomCamera.js (JavaScript Interface)

```javascript

import { NativeModules } from 'react-native';

const { CustomCamera } = NativeModules;
```

```
const openCamera = () => {
  CustomCamera.openCamera(
    (message) => {
      console.log(message); // Success callback
    },
    (error) => {
      console.error(error); // Error callback
    }
  );
};

export default openCamera;
```

- **Explanation**: This JavaScript function calls the openCamera method of the **CustomCameraModule**. It handles both the success and error responses from the native code.

Integrating Complex Native UI Components into Your App

Native UI components can be integrated into your React Native app when a custom design or functionality is required. React Native's bridge allows you to create native views that can be embedded directly into the React Native layout.

365

1. Creating a Custom Native View (Android and iOS)

For example, let's say you need a custom native map view for location-based apps.

- For **Android**, you would create a native **MapView** component using Google Maps or any other library.
- For **iOS**, you could use **MapKit** or third-party libraries to create a map view.

Once created, these native views are rendered in React Native using `requireNativeComponent`, which is a special React Native API for rendering native views.

```javascript
import React from 'react';
import { requireNativeComponent } from 'react-native';

const NativeMapView = requireNativeComponent('NativeMapView');

const App = () => {
  return (
    <NativeMapView style={{ flex: 1 }} />
  );
};
```

```
export default App;
```

- **Explanation**: In this example, the `NativeMapView` is a custom native view that is rendered directly in React Native. The native code for the `NativeMapView` component would be implemented separately for Android and iOS.

Real-World Example: Integrating a Custom Native Camera Module for Image Processing

In this real-world example, we'll integrate a custom camera module that can capture images and perform basic image processing (e.g., resizing or applying filters). We will use the native **camera** APIs on both Android and iOS to capture images, and then pass the image data back to the React Native app for further processing.

1. Camera Integration (Android and iOS)

- On **Android**, we'll use the **Camera API** to open the camera, capture an image, and pass the image URI back to JavaScript.
- On **iOS**, we'll use **UIImagePickerController** to capture the image and return it to JavaScript.

367

2. Image Processing with React Native

Once the image is captured, you can use React Native libraries such as **react-native-image-resizer** or **react-native-fs** for image processing and file handling.

```bash
npm install react-native-image-resizer
```

Here's how you would resize an image:

```javascript
import ImageResizer from 'react-native-image-resizer';

const processImage = async (uri) => {
  const newImage = await ImageResizer.createResizedImage(uri, 800, 800, 'JPEG', 80);
  console.log('Resized image URI:', newImage.uri);
};
```

- **Explanation**: After capturing the image using the custom camera module, we resize the image using **react-native-image-resizer** before displaying or saving it.

368

Conclusion

In this chapter, we explored how to extend React Native with **advanced native integration** and **native UI components**. We covered the following:

- **Native modules**: How to create custom native modules for accessing platform-specific features, such as a custom camera module.
- **Native UI components**: How to integrate complex native views (such as a custom map view) into your React Native app.
- **Real-world example**: Building a custom native camera module for image processing, allowing you to capture and process images in your React Native app.

By integrating native modules and custom views, you can unlock platform-specific features and create highly optimized, feature-rich applications. In the next chapter, we will cover best practices for performance optimization and debugging in React Native.